Burke

# Magdalena and Balthasar

An Intimate Portrait of Life
in 16th-Century Europe
Revealed in the Letters of
a Nuremberg Husband and Wife
and Illuminated by

## STEVEN OZMENT

SIMON AND SCHUSTER
NEW YORK

Library of Congress Cataloging in Publication Data

Paumgartner, Magdalena Balthasar, 1555–1642.
  Magdalena and Balthasar.

  Bibliography: p.
    1. Paumgartner, Magdalena Balthasar, 1555–1642—
Correspondence.   2. Paumgartner, Balthasar, 1551–1600—
Correspondence.   3. Germany—Social life and customs.
I. Paumgartner, Balthasar, 1551–1600.   II. Ozment,
Steven E.   III. Title.
DD177.P38A4   1986      943'.03      86–15546
ISBN: 0-671-62440-7

# ❧ACKNOWLEDGMENTS

This book could not have been written without the assistance of several people. There are, first of all, the librarians and archivists of Nuremberg: Gerhard Bott, Director of the Germanisches Nationalmuseum; Frau Schmidt-Fölkersamb, Archivoberrätin, Frau Gusti Schneider-Hiller, H. Maué, and Herr Bartelmess of the Staatarchiv Nürnberg; and Dr. Frhr. von Brandenstein of the Landeskirchliches Archiv. I have also received very helpful assistance from my linguistically gifted colleagues Matthias Senger and James Hankins. No author could receive more helpful advice from an editor than I received from Jane Isay. Lastly, there is my wife, Andrea, whose good judgment and support always improve my work.

*For Amanda and Emma*

# ❦ INTRODUCTION

Perhaps most books begin more or less accidentally. This one surely did. Some years ago I had begun research for a study of cultural change in central Europe during the sixteenth century. Since I believe that the direct accounts of contemporaries are the bedrock of historical knowledge, a key question in my mind was what people who had lived through a great part of the century considered its character to be. As autobiographical writing had emerged on a large scale in the second half of the century, sources were plentiful in the form of house books, family chronicles, diaries, letters, and travelogues. I gathered a dozen or so such sources and began to make my way through them—works like the 1572 autobiography of the Basel publisher and schoolmaster Thomas Platter, who had lived through the Reformation in Switzerland, and the diary of the Augsburg merchant Ulrich Krafft, who spent three years in debtors' prison (1574–77) in Tripoli when the Manlich firm he represented there went bankrupt. Whereupon I picked up a collection of 169 letters written by a Nuremberg merchant and his fiancée and later wife between the years 1582 and 1598. The letters had been transcribed from the archives of the Germanisches Nationalmuseum in Nuremberg and pub-

lished in 1895. The editor, Georg Steinhausen, a special-
ist in the history of the German letter, sidetracked me
immediately with his brief rationale for making the letters available to scholars.

Today [he complained] an impartial observer must
conclude that the publication of letters of political and particularly of literary interest threatens
to become excessive. The very reverse, however,
may be said of letters of purely cultural interest.
Today, an interest in letters seems to be deemed
justified only when the letters concern matters of
some political importance, when the writer or ad-
dressee is an outstanding statesperson, say, a prince
or a princess, or when he or she has played a role
in the history of literature and has gained a place
in intellectual history.

Steinhausen went on to defend his publication of the
letters of two "purely average people of no literary sig-
nificance whatsoever"; their very obscurity, he believed,
made them historically interesting. Here, already in the
late nineteenth century, the "new" history was scolding
the "old." However, to no avail. Apart from a German-
ist's linguistic analysis of the letters, Professor Steinhausen's labor has been virtually ignored for ninety
years.

Intrigued historiographically by the editor's complaint,
I plunged into the letters, spurred on by the rare prospect of hearing two ordinary, but literate, people speak
their minds intimately and at length over a sixteen-year
period. Thus began my long acquaintance with the Nuremberg merchant Balthasar Paumgartner (1551–1600)
and his wife, Magdalena Behaim (1555–1642).

As they were not peasants and had means, I had no
illusions that I had stumbled upon the silent voice of
Europe's common man. On the other hand, these were
also no aristocrats of any historical accomplishment. Indeed, had the pair not been members of families impor-

tant in the political and commercial history of their city, their letters would not have been preserved in the Behaim family archives in Nuremberg's German National Museum. As it was customary in the larger German towns since the late fifteenth century to educate girls to vernacular literacy, Magdalena could read and write and reckon a bit. Her language is the vernacular of late medieval Nuremberg, difficult at times for a modern reader, but lively and creative, as indeed is she. I do not know of another example in the sixteenth century of a woman speaking her mind so freely and so fully on such a variety of issues. Balthasar, on the other hand, had been prepared for the merchant's trade since youth. His language, as his bearing, tends to be that of the professional businessman, clearer and more precise than Magdalena's and always, but never only, to the point.

In attempting to recreate their world and set the letters in a proper historical context, I have organized my book thematically around their own preoccupations and allowed them to interpret their lives in their own words. Each chapter, like each letter, contains the whole, but focused on one of their several major interests. Obviously these were two people tossed about by the many powerful currents that swept late-sixteenth-century Nuremberg—political and social, economic and commercial, intellectual and religious, physical and epidemiological. But they are also individuals who swim against the great streams of nature and culture. We meet them, first, simply as lovers, as a couple who live intimately in their own private world. Year after year, in a variety of ways, love and endearment fill their letters. We come to know them also as close business partners. During Balthasar's frequent absences from Nuremberg, Magdalena expertly, diplomatically, and not least profitably managed his affairs. They are parents of an only child whom they rear for almost a decade to an excruciating youthful death. Particularly in parenthood they discover the peaks and valleys of their lives. They are both what modern slang would call "health nuts," devotees of purgative medicine, doggedly, defiantly, occasionally pitiably in search of effective prophylaxis against the raging maladies and diseases of their age. Finally, we discover them to be two people in a love-hate relationship with God, their Afflicter and their Redeemer.

The weekly letters give us only a glimpse of their lives—rarely more than six months out of each year when Balthasar is pursuing his business in Lucca or at the Frankfurt or Leipzig spring or fall fair. On one or two occasions, we are unable to follow an engrossing episode to its conclusion, as the correspondence simply ends and the episode resolves itself before the correspondence resumes. On the other hand, the letters deal with the things that mattered most in their lives. Where the information is occasionally limited, or the perspective only partial, the matters addressed remain vital, the *pars valentior*. They are letters from the heart.

# *I*

# A CITY
# OF MERCHANTS

"The German Venice": that title, bestowed on Nuremberg in the sixteenth century by foreign merchants, epitomized the city's position as a major European commercial center. William Smith (d. 1618), an Englishman resident in the city from the early 1570s to the early 1590s, the approximate years of our story, included proverbial encomia to Nuremberg merchants in his description of the city for Lord Burghley. "The city is furnished with such store of merchants," he wrote, "that it is a common proverb in Germany: 'The merchants of Nuremberg, the Lords of Ulm, and the Citizens of Augsburg.' Also there is a rhyme, 'The Nuremberg hand Deceaves every land.' "

Geography was the handmaiden of Nuremberg's success. Sited strategically in south-central Germany between the Main and the Danube, the city provided convenient overland access to the major waterways and trade routes of central Europe (the river Pegnitz, on which it squarely sat, was too narrow and too shallow to be a major shipping lane). Regensburg lay sixty-five miles to the southeast, Augsburg ninety miles to the south, Ulm ninety-five miles to the southwest, Erfurt 130 miles to the north, Frankfurt 135 miles to the north-

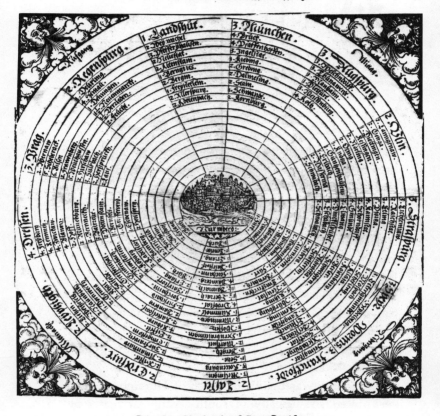

A Nuremberg travel chart by Georg Kreidlein, printed in
1560, indicates the number of miles between Nuremberg and
thirteen other major cities, including the intermediate stops.
One German mile equals five English miles.
Reprinted by permission of the Germanisches Nationalmuseum,
Nuremberg.

west, Prague 170 miles to the east, and Leipzig 180 miles to the northeast. These distances could take weeks to cover because of road and weather conditions, the detours created when highwaymen, soldiers, or outbreaks of the plague cut routes, and the delays created when one entered a new territory (during the 135-mile journey from Nuremberg to Frankfurt, a merchant crossed six different territorial jurisdictions). Also, merchants did business in the intermediate small towns and villages along their routes. Once, when Balthasar made it to Leipzig within five weeks of his departure, Magdalena congratulated him on the good management of his affairs. Nuremberg also had extraordinary connections with the great mercantile capitals of Italy, whose firms expanded their branches in the city during the second half of the century.

Together with slightly larger Augsburg and Cologne, Nuremberg was one of sixteenth-century Germany's most populous cities, governing a twenty-five-square-mile territory. A particularly detailed census taken in 1450, when the city was under siege, counted 20,219 permanent residents and 9,912 fugitive peasants, a total population within its walls exceeding 30,000. Over a century and a half later, in 1622, a household census counted 8,939 burgher and 1,130 nonburgher families, a total population of between 40,000 and 50,000, if we allow four to five members per household. Artisan families occupied more than half of these households. Their sizable presence in the city and the vitality they lent it were dramatically attested in 1592 when a public celebration drew no fewer than 5,500 artisans representing 277 different crafts and trades. During the lifetime of our Balthasar, Nuremberg's population probably ranged around 35,000.

Nuremberg was a "free imperial" city, one of the most important in the Holy Roman Empire. This meant that it owed allegiance to only one overlord, the Hapsburg

Emperor. It was obligated to provide him with hospitality during his infrequent visits and to meet certain imperial tax and military assessments. The arrangement left the city virtually autonomous as far as its own internal political life was concerned. The city magistrates shrewdly maintained good relations with the Emperor, despite their dissent from his religious policy. Firmly Lutheran since the 1520s, Nuremberg never joined the Protestant Schmalkaldic League formed in the 1530s to check the Catholic Emperor, nor did it furnish any troops to the League, but it did contribute over the years the handsome sum of 80,000 gulden to the League's support. The city also remained aloof from the Lutheran Formula of Concord, a conservative confessional alignment of Lutheran cities and territories after 1577. Because Nuremberg was clever enough to both agree and disagree with Catholic Emperor and Protestant prince alike, the city's service to other lords did not prevent it from remaining its own master.

A group of about thirty aristocratic families ruled the city. The Englishman Smith admiringly describes them as the "prudent and sage Counsel of the gentility . . . through whose politic and wise government the people are kept in quietness, due awe, and obedience." Forty-two representatives made up the ruling Small Council. Of these, thirty-four were patricians and eight were commoners representing the major trades (a brewer, a tailor, a leatherer, a butcher, a baker, a clothmaker, a goldsmith, and a furrier). These thirty-four occupied the major administrative and judicial offices of the city, from the "lords of war" to those of mere bridges and streets. A Large Council, numbering four hundred by 1590, also existed. Its main function was to ratify and help implement the policies of the Small Council.

Nuremberg was a wealthy city, and great disparity existed in income levels. When the Council assessed taxes in 1568, it found 416 burghers, 6 to 8 percent of the inhabitants, with total wealth in excess of 5,000 gulden, 240 of these with wealth in excess of 10,000 gulden. As 50 gulden was a barely livable annual wage in the late sixteenth century, these were respectable sums. To take an example close to our story, in the year of his first marriage (1549), Magdalena's father, Paul Behaim, put his basic household expenses, including two maids, a cook, and a male servant, at 2,365 gulden. A journeyman in the cloth industry, by contrast, earned a mere 100 gulden a year, while a master got at least twice that.

The city attempted to control the number of people at the lower economic levels by setting a high minimal fee for citizenship (100 gulden, more than triple what, for example, Nördlingen charged) and by requiring a minimum amount of property, the level of which varied from profession to profession. A dye-master, for example, in order to set up shop in Nuremberg with all the rights and privileges of citizenship, had to have total wealth of 350 gulden—200 of this in propertied wealth, 100 for citizenship, and 50 for a craft license. The minimum propertied wealth required of a linen worker, by contrast, was only 50 gulden. The city remained home also to a sizable underclass of noncitizens—day laborers, pieceworkers in the service industries, transient aides to artisans and merchants—who lived from hand to mouth and probably made up a good 10 percent of the population. In time of crisis (plague, war, or famine) a third of the city's population might require basic material assistance.

While the vast majority of Nurembergers were locked into their economic lots, mobility did exist. A striking example is the magnificent Italian merchant Bartholomaeus Viatis, at his death Nuremberg's and possibly Germany's richest man. Viatis, a native Venetian, started out earning twenty-six pfennigs a day as a novice apprentice in Nuremberg; when he died he left a fortune of 1,125,341 gulden. Like the great majority of successful Nuremberg merchants, he made his fortune conservatively, in direct trade, clear of high-risk banking and lending. In 1593, our Balthasar acted as middleman for the transfer of 12,000 gulden to various Nuremberg merchants, including 3,000 to Viatis. The merchants of Nuremberg had a reputation for frugality and modesty in lifestyle. They mixed daily with ordinary townspeople, whose pleasures and values they shared, and took their turns guarding the walls as readily and regularly as any commoner. Merchants received no favored treatment when taxes were assessed or when they broke the law. The Englishman Smith was amazed to find only two notary publics in the city, clear testimony, he believed, to the basic honesty and dependability of the Nurembergers. "So true and just are they in their dealings, that their word is as much as an obligation. . . . If you lose a purse of money in the street, ring bracelet or such like, you shall be sure to have it again." What most impressed Smith, a Londoner, about Nuremberg was its good order and cleanliness. He counted 528 paved streets and lanes, thirteen public hot-water baths, 118 water wells and conduits "wherewithall almost every man's house is served," and twelve active churches and chapels (another fifteen stood inactive, silent witnesses to the Reformation). Smith also found it striking that no dunghills existed along the streets, "only in certayne odd by corners," and that the people did not urinate freely in the streets. Urine and other refuse could not be thrown out of the houses until after ten o'clock at night, on penalty of fine and imprisonment. While each family was allowed one pig in its yard, the animal had to be placed in a stall outside the city when it became half a year old. Perhaps the stern punishments readily meted out for crimes also had something to do with the good order and honest character Smith ascribed to Nurembergers. Convicted thieves were hung if they were not citizens and beheaded if they

*A bird's-eye view of Nuremberg, most civil and orderly of
cities, around the time of Magdalena's death, by Matthais
Merian.*
From *Topographia Franconiae . . . durch Matthais Merian*
(Frankfurt a.M., 1655; photo-reprint edition, 1962). Reprinted by
permission of Johannes Stauda Verlag, Kassel.

were. Arsonists were burned at the stake. Those guilty of swearing false oaths had two joints of their foremost fingers removed, while blasphemers lost their tongues. Lesser crimes brought whipping and banishment. In the second half of the sixteenth century, Nuremberg entered a gradual decline as a trading and manufacturing center. Europe's great trading centers had shifted to the Atlantic seaboard, away from the Adriatic and the Mediterranean, to which Nuremberg provided convenient access. Lisbon, Antwerp, and later Amsterdam displaced Venice and Genoa as western Europe's main trading ports. New protectionist policies, reflecting the political centralization of nation-states and their growing competition, curtailed Nuremberg's markets, especially in France and the Netherlands. Within the city itself, Italian firms, eighteen of which had resident representatives by 1574, skimmed off much of the spice and precious cloth trade, key items in Balthasar's business. Nuremberg's famous penchant for moral order and discipline also played a role, for the city's conscientious supervision of mercantile activity drove some merchants to relocate in cities with freer trade policies and greater willingness to bend laws—Augsburg in particular.

A series of major epidemics that struck between 1560 and 1584 also sent the city reeling in the second half of the century. Plague killed an astonishing 9,186 children over the four-year period between 1561 and 1564. In 1570, some 1,600 children died of smallpox. Between 1573 and 1576 there were 6,500 deaths from plague and dysentery, while spotted fever (measles or smallpox) took 5,000 lives in 1585. During these twenty-five years, Nuremberg suffered population losses that it took a generation to replenish.

The artistic and cultural life of the city also declined in the second half of the century. During the first half, Nuremberg had been the center of the German Renaissance and Reformation, and the art of Albrecht Dürer and the poetry of Hans Sachs reached an international audience. Such preeminence could not be sustained, despite the brilliant goldwork of Wenzel Jamnitzer and the versatile prints of Jost Amman. When Nuremberg's wealthy merchants collected art in the 1570s and '80s, they competed for the masters of the first half of the century. There was a notable architecture (especially magnificent private town houses), portraiture, and sculpture during the second half of the century, but its influence remained local. The artistic and cultural life of the city had reached a plateau—a high one, to be sure, but not the heights of the age of Dürer.

## ❧ THE BEHAIMS AND THE PAUMGARTNERS

Behaim and Paumgartner are important names in Nuremberg's political, commercial, and cultural life. The Behaims had been established merchants in Nuremberg since the thirteenth century, the Paumgartners since the late fifteenth, when family members migrated from Augsburg to expand their business. Magdalena's and Balthasar's kin shaped a considerable part of Nuremberg's sixteenth-century history. Magdalena's father, Paul (d. 1568), was a senior burgomaster and a captain general in the 1550s and 1560s, and in 1561 he led the city's delegation to the congress in Naumberg where Lutheran territories, preparing for talks with Catholics at the Council of Trent, reaffirmed the oldest Lutheran confession, the Augsburg Confession. Magdalena's brother Paul (d. 1621) served the city as a junior burgomaster in the 1580s and '90s, while her brother Friedrich (d. 1613) was superintendent (*Pfleger*) over Gräfenburg and Hilpoldstein. Her siblings (she was the eldest of eight, all of whom she outlived) married into several of Nuremberg's most politically influential and commercially successful families.

Apart from the fact that Magdalena was educated to vernacular literacy and rarely traveled far beyond Nuremberg, we know little about her life during the years before her marriage. The same may be said for the years after her marriage. She was forty-five when Balthasar died, and she lived another forty-two years before her own death. The family genealogy indicates that she never remarried. One inference about her activity during these silent years may be drawn from her letters to her husband. She was very close to the members of her family, involved in both their private and business lives. Such intimacy was perhaps influenced by the fact that she was the eldest, although she, her siblings, and her in-laws seem also genuinely to have liked one another.

Balthasar's grandfather Caspar (d. 1523) and his father, Balthasar, Sr. (d. 1594), were members of the Large Council. They also served as city planners (Caspar as *Baumeister*, Balthasar as *Baurichter*) and superintendents in neighboring territories (Caspar over Kronburg Steinbruch, Balthasar over Altdorf). Balthasar's famous relatives Bernhard and Hieronymus were key figures in the city's political life for almost half a century. Bernhard died a member of the Seven, the government's privy council, in 1549. Hieronymus guided Nuremberg through the Reformation. A friend of Luther and Melanchthon, Hieronymus had been the first to whom Luther offered the hand of the renegade nun Katherine von Bora whom he himself finally married. At the time of his death in 1565, Hieronymus stood out among the powerful Three who ran the city. His son and our Balthasar's (personally distant) contemporary, Hieronymus, Jr., was curator of the Altdorf Academy, a school for patrician children founded in 1575 that evolved into a university in the seventeenth century. This Hieronymus died as first *Losunger*, the city's recognized highest official, in 1602. In 1592, marriage again linked the Behaims and the Paumgartners, this time at the highest political level, when Hieronymus' daughter Rosina married Magdalena's brother Paul.

Balthasar also had an impressive pedigree on his mother's side. Helena Paumgartner (d. 1567) was a Scheurl. Her family, like the Paumgartners, had settled Nuremberg in the 1460s. Her father, Albrecht (d. 1530), was a successful merchant, and her uncle Christoph was the renowned humanist and jurist who conducted the disputations in the 1520s that made the Reformation official (although he himself later returned to the old church).

A medallion in the German National Museum bearing Balthasar's likeness dates his death in 1601 and describes him as being thirty-eight years of age at the time; a contemporary portrait conveys the identical information. However, all the authoritative genealogies, including an etching of his family tree, date his death in July 1600, without venturing either his birth date (in Altdorf, near Nuremberg) or his age at death. There are good reasons to challenge the accuracy of thirty-eight as Balthasar's age at death. Not only would this make him an incredible nine-year-old apprentice in Nuremberg, but he would also have been only twenty at the time of his marriage to Magdalena in 1583, well under the legal minimum age (twenty-five) for men to marry without parental permission, and his wife's junior by six years. A check of the baptismal book of Nuremberg's St. Sebald Church has definitely established his birthdate in 1551. He was baptized on February 19 of that year, a day or two after his birth. "Walthasar Paumgartner filius Walthasar—19 Februarii," reads the entry.

By comparison with many of their kin, Magdalena and Balthasar were very dim lights, ordinary members

of extraordinary families. Balthasar never held or as-
pired to any public office, and his financial success was
hard won and modest. His once-in-a-lifetime indulgence
was a Polish wolf coat, while Magdalena could rhapso-
dize over a bolt of silk; the high life for her was a few
days with her husband in an Augsburg inn. Although
Balthasar managed to purchase a small estate in Holenstein in late 1596 and to escape the merchants' harsh
regimen after 1597, he remained a man who had always
to count his gulden.

It is the obscurity and ordinary qualities of our couple
that give their story an advantage, for they are rich in
frustration and hope, the real stuff of history. With their
eyes fixed on the morrow, they are always game, search-
ing, ready to experiment. And, best of all, they tell all.

## II

# ʃLOVERS

Balthasar Paumgartner and Magdalena Behaim were betrothed in October 1582 and married six months later, in April 1583. During their engagement, when passions were strong, they exchanged letters between Lucca, where Balthasar's business had taken him, and Nuremberg, where Magdalena awaited his return. Eleven of these letters have survived, eight from Balthasar, three from Magdalena. The lovers followed the epistolary conventions of the day, so the letters occasionally express love and affection in highly stylized formulas which a casual reader might mistake for insincerity or, at least, a lack of imagination. The couple greet each other, for instance, as "most beloved" or, setting piety ahead of desire, "after God, my heart's dearest treasure." Typically the letters bear solemn pledges of "true, friendly, benevolent, unending devotion." They can conclude with "one hundred thousand friendly and sincere greetings." Balthasar self-effacingly describes himself as "a poor reluctant writer, who prefers to say his words in person rather than write them." "Pay me a visit with a little letter," he will lovingly plead. Or he can blossom forth: "May God in His grace preserve us and bring us soon together again in our little garden of joy."

Magdalena receives all Balthasar's letters with "longing and heartfelt joy." A letter from him at Christmastime becomes "a true gift from the Christ Child." Magdalena later treasured a letter she received in the first year of their marriage on the day of her bleeding (she bled herself at regular intervals during the year in the belief that it ensured her good health) as "the best bleeding-day gift I could receive." She folds flowers from their garden into her letters to him. On one occasion she included a string for Balthasar to bind about his wrist as a token of their "friendly bond" with each other, a custom connected with Epiphany, the commemoration of the visit of the kings of the Orient, in friendship, to the manger of Christ. With the solemnity of a pastor addressing his congregation, Balthasar opens his Christmas letter of the same year by wishing Magdalena "a Happy New Year through Jesus Christ, the newborn child, our only Savior, Redeemer, and Sanctifier."

Such terms and acts of endearment might suggest artifice and contrivance to some readers. This "new chancery style" of writing, allegedly reflecting the "servile spirit of the age of Reformation," has been noticed particularly in Balthasar's letters by the scholar who first transcribed them. But the formulaic expressions of love are really just the trappings on letters of real intimacy. They frame the genuine expressions of love between two individuals whose private lives remained remarkably free and spontaneous—lovers, even in the modern sense of the term.

## ❦ INTIMACY

BALTHASAR TO MAGDALENA
*15 December 1582, in Lucca*

My honest, good, true, friendly, dearest, closest bride:
I have at 12:00 this night received with great longing

your letter of November 11. As I had carefully considered and calculated the mail delivery with which your reply to my letter must come, I waited with longing for a letter last Sunday; anticipating it, I did not leave the house the entire day. But how just it would have been to me, had you not written as soon as you did!

The news that all are well is received most happily. I and all my associates here are also, praise God, still well. May it be God's will to keep us in his grace and help us soon to come happily together again in our little garden of joy.

I am truly happy to hear that you have already visited my old Aunt Scheurl several times and that she was so friendly to you, which I never doubted she would be. Please continue to visit her when there is opportunity, and cultivate her counsel in various matters. I know she enjoys such attention and that she is especially well pleased when someone places their trust in her and takes her advice. She also wants us to think well of her and, when possible, to turn to her as to a friend. Although she is of little benefit to us, she is also the kind of person who will never do us any harm. But you already know well how to stroke the tail of the fox, of that I have no doubt.

Dearest one, with this letter you will have discovered the reason, and therein also my excuse, for being so slow and rather irregular in my writing. As far as I can tell from your present letter, you have not yet received such clarification from me. Matters were such that had I managed now and then to write to you while I was on the road, I would have brought you little joy and much worry. For as long as I am traveling and wagering on good fortune and not yet home, I have no assurance whatsoever that the strong prohibitions against travelers issued because of plague will allow me to enter the towns through which I must pass and make my way back to you. I do not want to add to your worries with news of such difficulties.

But if you have often asked why and have been surprised that you have received no letter from me, the same has certainly also been true for me here. Every

Sunday, when the mail usually arrives, there has been no end to the question in my mind why you have not written to me, and I have also pondered why you will not write to me until you have first received a letter from me. So let this anger between us end!

Most dearest love, I will await your answer to this letter here. Thereafter, you need not write to me again in Lucca, for around the end of January I will have to travel on business to other places and towns en route to Modena and Reggio, and for this reason your letters may no longer find me here. Too much is presently unsettled in our business to know for sure if I will depart so soon. I desire to go, but all too often and far too long I am prevented by many things beyond my control. If I could now complete one most important matter in which our firm has not a little invested, how quickly I would turn the other matters over to my brother and the staff here and be on my way! I am trusting and hoping in Almighty God that next January nothing will prevent my planned departure.

Meanwhile there is plenty for me to do here. Over the holiday I am going to Florence, which is forty miles away, but I will be returning here in three or four days. Meanwhile, trust that on my return from Florence my health may, praise God, be good and that I will have recovered from my wearisome journey, for I will return here beaten and exhausted. Take care not to let yourself be tormented by many vain worries over things which in the end you can do nothing about. You may be sure that as soon as my affairs here are settled, I will not tarry here one hour, but (God willing) may hope to be with you there even sooner than you and I now think. May dear God grant that hope soon and happily!

I am certainly distressed to hear about the long, grievous pestilence you are having. Others there have written to me that it has abated somewhat and that cold weather is on the doorstep.* I hope to almighty God

* Cold weather was welcomed in times of pestilence because it inhibited spread of the disease.

that it has not posed any further danger. Here we have had almost beautiful bright weather for five weeks. Many others would not say so, as at this time of the year it customarily mostly rains (presently the rain is steady) and many are surprised by the beautiful weather.

I had learned already before your letter from cousin Andreas Imhoff in Venice of the blessed departure from life of the good and pious Sebastian Imhoff in Lyon. Wilhelm Kress, who was with him in Lyon, suffered not a little with him. May the Almighty be to him as to all of us gracious and merciful and grant him after this life eternal life! Amen.

I had also learned before your letter that old Matthew Fetzer is a bridegroom. However, his bride, and the Rosina whom Dr. Wolff is marrying, are unknown to me.

Wilhelm Kress, whom I have put up here in good quarters, and brother Jörg both again send their sincere greetings and thank you kindly for thinking of them.

When you see Frau Lochner, indicate to her that I will do my best to get the crimson satin lining and the bicolored double taffeta. I had already ordered the lining before I got your letter.

Otherwise, apart from my work, I lead a truly boring life without any diversions whatsoever, save for a two-week visit here of players who performed every evening for four hours after sunset into the night. Among them was a woman who could (as one is accustomed to say) "speak and ride." I wish to God you could have seen her, for you would certainly have marveled. I passed some time watching the plays, but such things come to an end. After the Christmas holidays other players will come, but they are no match for the plays you have in St. Martha's and the Dominican cloister there. But I cannot sufficiently describe how eloquent and skillful the women in such plays here are, especially the one who was just here. If you have not seen it for yourself, you cannot believe it. Without doubt, they have studied many storybooks and must be well taught.

Among other things in your letter, you announce that I should not again wait so long to write to you: "who knows [you say] but that I may find you more than once among the bad women who hold sway there!" By saying such a thing you have disturbed me not a little and raised all kinds of strange thoughts in my mind. If dear God cannot immediately reconcile us, I still trust he will spare us this time and help guide us joyfully back together again in our little chamber or flower garden. We are all in his hands, and if I do not place my entire hope in him, I must constantly worry that misfortune will befall me. I am hoping for the best from him and you should, too, in the end letting him rule.

Dearest and closest, I don't know what more to write you at this time. Only that I thank you most sincerely for the little flower you have sent me from our garden. I am carefully preserving it for your sake. May I kindly ask you to give my sincere greetings and best wishes to your brother Paul, your sister, and to Katherina Imhoff and Magdalena Held. And for you, dearest Magdale, many hundred thousand friendly and sincere greetings! I commend you in trust to the grace of the loving God.

*Your true, loving bridegroom,*
*Balthasar Paumgartner the Younger*

On October 24, 1582, in his first letter to Magdalena after settling into the family house in Lucca, Balthasar recalled the evening they had parted and his inability at that time to anticipate how difficult their separation would be. "I have not been able to free my mind of the way you swooned in my arms upstairs in your little chamber," he writes; "since then, few, very few, hours have passed when I have not thought of you." These have included his sleeping as well as his waking hours, for he claims to have "dreamed constantly" of Magdalena since his first night in Lucca.

Each is sensitive, often to a fault, to the frequency of other's communications during this their first separation, which would last for six months, from October 1582 to March 1583. After Balthasar at last receives Magdalena's first letter, written November 11 and unfortunately no longer extant, he confides to her in his return letter of December 15 that in his longing he had calculated the time it would take for her to receive his earlier letter and respond, and he had stayed home the entire day on which he guessed her letter would arrive. Of course he was disappointed, but it served him right, he acknowledges, because, as Magdalena has evidently complained, he had also not written to her as promptly as he might have. Anticipating trouble, Balthasar in his first letter had attempted to explain his delay in writing. Why had he not written while en route to Lucca? Because he did not want to disturb her with news of closed roads and forced detours or bore her with accounts of frustrated or lost business opportunities. Fear of plague often moved townspeople to blockade the roads into their towns and divert travelers; this was a common hazard of the merchant trade. Balthasar neglected to mention, however, that he had waited a full five days after his arrival in Lucca before setting pen to paper.

Magdalena did not accept Balthasar's explanations; she scolded him as if she felt betrayed. Balthasar replied with his own complaint: she may have wondered why he had not written, but so might he wonder about her. On many a Sunday, apparently mail day in Lucca, he waited in vain for a letter. And why did she have to wait to write to him only after he had first written to her? "So let this anger between us end!"

This was not a simple matter, because Magdalena suspected that Balthasar's delay indicated he was straying. Who knows, he paraphrases her letter as insinuating, but that she may find him frequenting the prostitutes there! If this was a joke, Balthasar thought it was in bad taste, and it left him "disturbed not a little" and planted "all kinds of strange thoughts" in his mind.

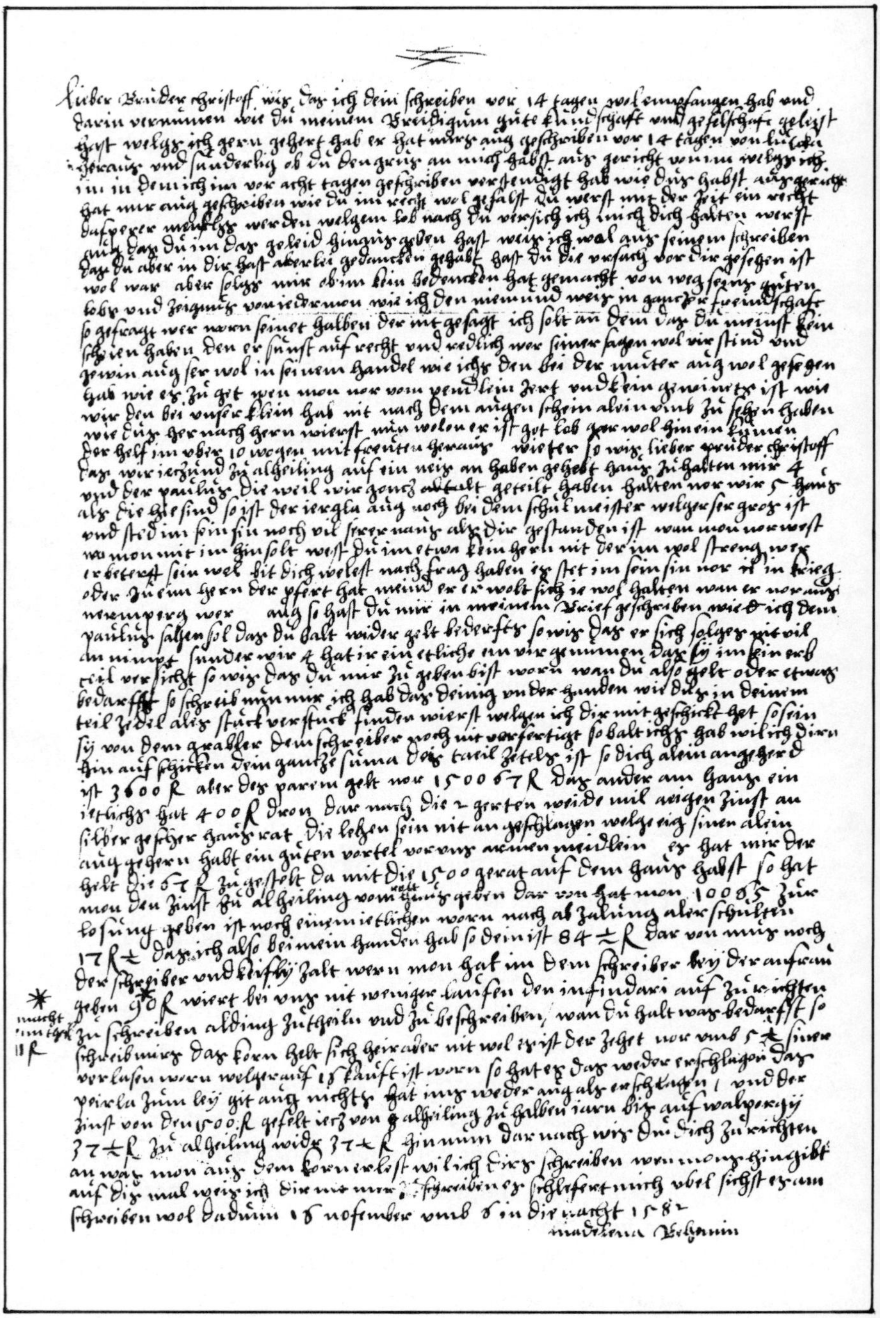

lieber bruder christoff wis das ich dein schreiben vor 14 tagen wol empfangen hab und
darin vernumen wie du meinem breitigum gute freindschaft und gesellschaft geleist
hast welches ich gern gehert hab er hat mir auch geschriben vor 14 tagen von lucka
heraus und sunderlich ob du den gemis an mich habst auch gericht vor im welches ich
im in dem ich im vor acht tagen geschriben verstendigt hab wie dir habst auch gewist
hat mir auch geschriben wie du im recht wol gefalst du werst mit der zeit ein recht
dapferer menlichs werden welchem lob nach du versich ich mich dich halten werst
auch das du im das geleid hinaus geben hast weis ich wol aus seinem schreiben
das du aber in dir hast aberlei gedancken gehabt hast du die ursach vor dir gesehen ist
wol war aber solches mir ob im kein bedencken hat gemacht von weg seines guten
lobs und zeignus von iederman wie ich den niemand weis in gantzer freindschaft
so gefragt wer wenn seinet halben der mir gesagt ich solt an dem das du meinst kein
scheien haben den er sunst auf recht und redlich wer seiner sachen wol versteind und
gewin auch ser wol in seinem handel wie ichs den bei der muter auch wol gesegen
hab wie er zu get wen man nur vom pendlein sagt und kein gemeinschaft ist wie
wir den bei unser klein hab mit nach dem augenschein allein und zu sehen halten
wie dus hernach hern wierst mir weler er ist got lob gar wol hinein kumen
der helf im uber 10 wegen mit freuden heraus wieter so wis lieber bruder christoff
das wir ietzund zu allerheiling auf ein neis an haben gehebt haus zu halten mir 4
und der paulus die weil wir gantz abtalt geteilt haben halten wir wir 5 haus
als die gesind so ist der ieglu auch noch bei dem schulmeister welches ser gros ist
und sted im sein sin noch vil sterrer nach als die gestanden ist wan man nur west
wo man mit im hin solt west du im etwan kein hern mit der im wol streng wer
er betret sein wol bit dich welest nach frag haben er stet im sein sin nor er in krieg
oder zu ein hern der pfert hat meint er er wolt sich ie wol halten wan er nor aus
nurmberg wer auch so hast du mir in meinem brief geschriben wie ich dem
paulus halten sol das du balt wider gelt bedorfts so wis das er sich solcher mit vil
an nimpt sunder wir 4 hat er ein etliche un vir gemumen das sy im kein erb
teil versicht so wis das du mir zu geben bist wan wan du also gelt oder etwas
bedarffst so schreib mir nur ich hab das deinig under handen wie du es in deinem
teil zedel als stuck verstuck finden wierst welchen ich dir mit geschickt het so sein
sy von dem grabler dem schreiber noch nit verfertigt so balt ichs hab wil ich dirn
hin auf schicken dein gantze suma des tail zetels ist so dich allein angehert
ist 3600 f aber der parn gelt wer 1500 67 f das ander am haus ein
ietlichs hat 400 f dran dar nach die 2 garten weide mil aigen zinst an
silber geschier haus rat die lehen sein nit an geschlagen welches ich seiner allein
auch gehern habt ein guten vortel vor uns armen meidlein er hat mir der
gelt die 67 f zu gestelt da mit die 1500 gerat auf dem haus habst so hat
man den zinst zu allerheiling vom haus geben dar von hat man 100 f zur
losung geben ist noch einem ietlichen worn nach al zalung aller schulden
17 f das ich also bei mein handen hab so dein ist 84 f dar von mir noch
der schreiber und briefs zalt wern man hat im dem schreiber bei der aufrain
geben 60 f wiert bei uns nit weniger laufen den infindari auf zu richten
zu schreiben alding zu teilen und zu beschreiben wan du balt was bedarffst so
schreib mirs das koren gelt sich heraus nit wol reist der zehet wor umb 5 f sinnen
verlasen wern welchs auf 15 kauft ist worn so hat es das weder eingeschlagen das
perlen zum bey git auch nichts hat mir weder auch als eingeschlagen und der
zinst von den 1500 f gefelt ietz von allerheiling zu halben iarn bis auf walburgis
37 f zu allerheiling wider 37 f hin num dar nach wis du dich zu richten
an was man aus dem koren erlost wil ich dirs schreiben wen man hingibt
auf dis mal weis ich dir nit mer zu schreiben es schlefert mich ubel sichst es am
schreiben wol dadum 15 nofember umb 8 in der nacht 1582
madalena behamin

* macht im teil 11 f

Reproduced by permission of the Germanisches Nationalmuseum, Hist. Archiv Rst. Nürnberg, Behaim File 80.

On his journey to Italy, Balthasar was accompanied part of
the way by Magdalena's younger brother, Christoph—apparently the first meeting between the two men. Something in
Balthasar's appearance or behavior raised concern about him
in Christoph's mind, which he shared in a letter with his sister. In this recently discovered letter of November 16, 1582,
Magdalena replies to Christoph in Augsburg. She defends
her bridegroom and gently scolds her brother as only a big
sister can (Magdalena was at least six years Christoph's
senior). The letter reads in part:

Dear brother Christoph. I received your letter two weeks
ago and was glad to learn from it that you have gotten to
know my bridegroom well and that you have also kept him
company. He also wrote me two weeks ago from Lucca and
[he] especially [wanted to know] whether you had extended
his greeting to me. When I wrote him last week, I informed
him that you had. He also said in his letter how pleased he
was with you and how [he believed that] in time you would
become an important man. You may expect me also to measure you by such praise. I also know from his letter that you
accompanied him [on his journey]. But since you have had
all kinds of thoughts about him, it is certainly true that you
know the cause. Such, however, has created no doubts in me
because of the high praise and respect he receives from everyone. I know of no one in our entire circle of friends who,
when asked about him, has said that I should have any concern about what you say. For he is otherwise upright and
honest, his reputation quite exceptional, and he is very successful in his business. I remember with Mother* how it
was when one is only consuming what one has and is taking
nothing in. We with our little [wealth], should not judge him
by external appearance alone.

In the latter part of the letter, Magdalena further reveals her
authority within the family by detailing for Christoph, who
has requested money, his share of the family inheritance and
taxes. In her account of the family inheritance, which is
being shared by all eight children (400 gulden each from the
family house, plus a share of the income from two gardens,
fields, a mill, rents, silver plate, and furniture), Magdalena
excludes some property, apparently long held in fief, which
may pass only to the four male heirs; she complains, half-
teasingly, half-seriously, that the boys at this point "have a
good advantage over us poor girls."

* Magdalena's mother died a widow on December 31, 1581.

Magdalena answered Balthasar on Christmas Day 1582. She is as usual both outspoken and self-effacing. She never hesitates to speak her mind; yet she never imposes her opinion directly on Balthasar. She has written without guile, and she denies altogether that she is angry with him. She also assumes that *he* is joking and not really angry. On the other hand, she also worries about causing a crisis in their relationship. "May God let us never again for a moment in our lives experience such a trial" as mutual anger! Magdalena's sensitivity to Balthasar's charge of anger may seem extreme, but it may reflect popular medical belief, to which she in most instances trustingly subscribed. Anger and melancholy were believed to be the two most life-threatening emotions—to be avoided at all costs, especially when plague threatened, because they most upset the humors and made a person vulnerable to illness and disease.

That her letter had made Balthasar anxious and put "strange thoughts" in his mind also distressed Magdalena. Her letters, she humbly confesses, are "completely bad, halting, childish writing," and she begs his forgiveness. Amid the reassurances of her love and longing, she reports an exchange with the recently widowed Frau Flexner, whose husband, a much older man, had apparently treated her badly. Attempting to console the woman, perhaps less for being a widow than for having been an abused wife, Magdalena expressed the hope that God would provide her with another husband who might make her forget her suffering. Frau Flexner responded to Magdalena's good wishes with laughter and teasing: Were you and Balthasar not already betrothed, I would not let you have him! Magdalena claims to have immediately thanked God that she and Balthasar were betrothed before Frau Flexner was widowed. Balthasar found the story very amusing.

Mollified, Balthasar, when he wrote again, dismissed his previous comments about anger as words written "in jest"; real anger was something he too would not joke about. However, he wanted her to know that he also understood what it meant to stand "emptyhanded" before a mailbox. The issue, as we will see, did not end here. The mannered sarcasm, "Having not heard from you, I have all the less to write to you," recurs in the correspondence.

Rare is the prenuptial letter that does not complain of boredom and unhappiness because of the separation. But we have to understand that, despite these protestations, their discontent was in fact neither constant nor unbearable. Balthasar, a workaholic, easily lost himself in the merchant's life of constant travel and bargaining; his business correspondence alone filled a sizable part of each day. He frequently traveled as his own purchasing agent throughout northern Italy and central Germany and played diplomat at the sixteenth-century equivalent of the businessman's lunch. He reports having "eaten with a great spoon"—banqueted royally—at the table of the local bishop and, with his brother Jörg, having stayed the night as the bishop's guest. Magdalena too led an active life. She was Balthasar's virtual agent in Nuremberg, busily informing relatives, friends, and local clients of the state of their orders and receiving, storing, and distributing merchandise as it arrived— activities that only increased after the marriage. Magdalena was also preoccupied with wedding preparations, especially the ordering of wedding clothes for herself, Balthasar, and attending servants and children. The necessary materials Balthasar sent ahead from Italy. In one letter, he worries that she is laboring too long over his wedding shirt, making sacrifices for him he neither deserves nor desires. "Don't overdo it and make it too expensive," he pleads.

Magdalena also played. In her New Year's Day 1583 letter, she reports having attended, after initial hesitation (ostensibly for propriety's sake), a New Year's Eve dance with Balthasar's sister, Helena. Although she claims to have "danced plenty," she assures Balthasar that her thoughts "were still constantly with you, my most dearest treasure!" Her dancing with other men evidently awakened no such feelings of jealousy or self-doubt in Balthasar as his delay in writing had awakened in her. His confidence in her devotion is steady, even supreme. Her not writing to him frequently enough irritates him, to be sure, but he sees it as merely thoughtlessness or a lack of discipline, never dreaming that it could be caused by diminished or straying affection. Her complaints about *his* infrequent writing annoy him far more than her lapses in writing. Both in his love life and in his business affairs, Balthasar was a man who attempted to live by a rule of patience. "With patience one comes far and overcomes much," he likes to tell Magdalena when either requires reassurance.

Privacy, finally, preoccupied the premarital correspondence of our separated pair. Neither wants anyone else to read their letters, and each reminds the other to be circumspect. Worried that a letter from Magdalena might arrive while he is away on business in Genoa and "fall into the hands of strangers," Balthasar makes arrangements for his brother to receive his mail and keep it safe. He frequently instructs her not to write to him at certain places after a certain date, as he will have departed and her letters will no longer find him there. Sharing Balthasar's concern, Magdalena plans her writing around his travel schedule, so that her letters may arrive in Lucca, Frankfurt, or Leipzig when Balthasar is likely to be there. This concern for privacy persisted through the early years of marriage. Magdalena especially blushed at the thought that anyone other than her husband might ever read her intimate revelations. In July 1584, when she was four months pregnant, she visited neighboring Altdorf, Balthasar's hometown, for the Peter-Paul Day Festival, the annual celebration of the founding of the Academy. At the conclusion of her account of the visit, she reveals in intimate detail in a postscript how a "sudden and inexplicable anxiety" had seized her upon her return.

My dear, I am getting more and more anxious. I don't know whether it is the result of the journey to Altdorf or what that disturbs me so. But I often think that God and time will tell. I am often so very frightened when this mood descends upon me. My heart's treasure, do not let this letter lie around for others to see: I would be embarrassed.

# ❧ DEVOTION

MAGDALENA TO BALTHASAR
*25 December 1582, in Nuremberg*

Honest, kind, dearest, closest bridegroom:
   With longing and heartfelt joy I received your letter on December 22 by our calendar* and from it learned that you and yours are well, which is the greatest happiness you can bring me. I take the letter and your health for a true Christmas present; they have made this holiday all the more joyful for me. I, my brother, and my sister are also in good health. May it be God's will so to keep all of us! Amen.
   Kind and dearest bridegroom, because the old year is past and this letter comes to you in the new, I wish you, my dearest, true bridegroom, a happy, new, and joyful year with every well-being, success, and blessing that is useful and good to you in body and soul! This I wish you from the bottom of my heart. Amen.

*In Italy, Balthasar follows the Gregorian Calendar, what he calls "the new calendar of his papal holiness," just issued in 1582 by Pope Gregory XIII and running ahead of the German calendar by ten days.

I thank you, my dearest treasure, for being so deeply concerned about the cold that you have provided me a long-sleeved vest, which I wear on your behalf and think of you. I assuredly know of no moment in the past when such [thoughtfulness] did not also occur. Therefore, I take the vest in gratitude until you return, which I hope with heartfelt joy God may grant soon.

Since, as I have gathered, I should not after this letter write again to you [in Lucca], my dearest bridegroom, I would very much like for you to let me know, if it is not difficult for you, whether after your trip to Mantua you will return again to Lucca or so soon be departing for home. I hope that during this time when I cannot write to you, you will have better opportunity to visit me with a letter. You write to me expressing the wish that we end the anger between us, but I know no such anger, and I take it you are joking. May God let us never again for a moment in our lives experience such a trial! I have written to you simply, with such longing for a letter from you that I thought of the saying "I was perishing before you came to me." I too hope, as you write, that God will guide us back together again in our little garden of joy and there keep us together for a long time.

The plague, praise God, has again abated with the arrival of cold weather.

Now you also write me that apart from your work you are having a completely boring time. I believe you; I feel it also with myself. I must do my chores, but only then are my thoughts not of you, my dearest treasure! Please, dearest bridegroom, tell me what you mean when you write your Aunt Scheurl that you are not only bored, which I believe, but that, whether you are here or there, you cannot stop worrying. Neither she nor I could understand what was causing you to worry so much. Would to God that I could help you bear this worry. How gladly I would do so, for this is not one of those vain worries about which one can in the end do nothing, like those you have written me to avoid. I was with Aunt Scheurl and she let me read your letter. She wanted to be a good companion to me, which she assuredly has never failed to be. She thanks you again for most kindly caring for me.

I want you also to know, dear, kind bridegroom, that your dear father has written to ask how we all are and he has also sent a buck and several fowl. I have written him back a little note sincerely thanking him, but I could think of nothing better to send along with it than a box of crackling, which will be good for his health. I wish to God that you could have helped me consume his gifts of food. But as that could not be, I invited in your place your sister, Paul Scheurl, Katherina Imhoff, and Magdalena Held. Paul Scheurl and Paul Ketzel had a prior dinner date with Grebner and therefore they came after dinner with Wilhelm Imhoff, Silvester Greser, and Paul Dietherr. Then began all kinds of fun and games for us and we were happy together.

This past week, on last Saturday, your [step]mother also sent me all kinds of sausages, as she had slaughtered several hogs. I always enjoy your family, for which I have you to thank.

I have also this week gone with your brother and his wife to the Frauen Gate. There, in a canal by the fish stream, a mighty, gushing fountain of pure brass with many waterfalls and spouts has been constructed. We have seen it and you will no doubt have heard about it because it has been built here for the King of Denmark.

I cannot let go unreported to you, kind, dear bridegroom, what [the recently widowed] Frau Flexner said to me when I condoled her with the hope that God would now compensate her suffering in another husband. The sentiment brought instant laughter rather than tears. She immediately smiled and said jokingly to me that if you were not already a bridegroom, she would never let me have you. I quickly said that I thanked God that you had become mine before she had become a widow! I told her I would write to you so that you might sometime decline her offer. She replied that she already knew in advance that you would only make fun of her when, with God's help, you returned.

It is true that people here have only scoffed at her when she cried over her [dead husband] Flexner. But she defends herself.

Kind and dearest treasure, with this letter I am sending a little string which you may bind [about your wrist] on my behalf and thereby think of me and be bound together with me in friendship. I hope this letter does not reach you three or four days after Epiphany (by our calendar), on which day people customarily bind themselves together with those who share their name. God willing, I should do the same, were it possible.

Otherwise, dear bridegroom, I do not have much news to report, except that Madgalena Löffelholz is Siegfried Pfinzing's bride. You will already doubtlessly know this and also the betrothal of the Minster pastor's daughter with Paltner, and Georg Henn with the widow Schweiker, and Lanzinger's son with Gelnaur's stepdaughter. . . .*

Otherwise, my dearest, most precious treasure, I know nothing more to write at this time. I would only beg that when it becomes possible that God again helps you make your way happily home, you will let us know from Augsburg the day you will be arriving here so that we may happily travel out to meet you, [I mean] only Paul Scheurl, his wife, your sister, and I. I ask you this lovingly; you will make me happy if you grant this request.

Aunt Lochner again sends her sincere greetings and thanks you for your efforts on her behalf. At the same time she left me a little bundle of felt from your order, which for your sake I politely accepted. I will never do anything with it; I was at the time just plain fainthearted.

I need not write you that I was terrified when pestilence broke out in three houses on our street up by the baker's and five people died.

I am now hoping that Almighty God will bring us

* Here the manuscript is illegible.

back together again in joy! Therefore, banish the
strange thoughts and the disturbance you write that I
have created in you, and forgive me. Do not let yourself
be troubled; be happy and of good cheer! May the Lord
God guide you happily back to me!

My brother Paul and my sisters send warm greetings
and wish you a happy new year and all things dear,
useful, and good to you. A happy new year to your
brother Jörg and also to Wilhelm Kress. I have heard
that they will be traveling with you.

Dearest bridegroom, many hundred thousand sincere
and friendly greetings and many happy and good wishes
from me for the new year! Treat kindly my completely
bad, halting, childish writing.

I am sending you with this letter the flower from our
garden, which I do not forget to do because I write to
you from there. I also pledge myself to you, my dear
treasure, with the first drink I take on holy Christmas
Day. Remember me also when you have the opportunity.

May Almighty God keep you.

*Magdalena Behaim, y.l.b.* [your loving bride]


Magdalena cared about her Balthasar and she let him
know it. She is on occasion almost poetic in conveying
her affection: "Every Wednesday, as I free myself to
write to you, I think how we now have one less week of
our lives to share." The state of his health is her constant preoccupation. "From one week to the next my
greatest joy is in learning how you are," she tells him.
"News of your good health is the best gift you can give
me my life long."

She insists on organizing his life from afar. His bad
habits of working late and eating poorly and irregularly
are constantly criticized. She has suggestions for his
Italian cook and she rejoices when he gets a more effi-

cient maid. She never tires of preaching the benefits of mineral water (both drinking it and bathing in it) and of regular bleeding. She urges caution and good sense when he travels, especially that he not take unnecessary risks to save "holy time" when he is returning home to her and is most tempted to rush.

She sends him clothing and food regularly. Anticipating his arrival in Frankfurt from Italy for the fall fair of 1584, she sends ahead a gray overcoat ("it may be cool there"), five shirts, four handkerchiefs, three hats, three pairs of socks, one pair of shoes, and one pair of lined green slippers. As late-night treats she includes sour cherries and both sweet and sour (that is, sugared and salted) crackling. Crackling was the food she sent most often to Balthasar and others. It traveled well, was tasty, provided lots of calories, and Magdalena believed it had definite medicinal benefits. On another occasion (September 1589) she writes to him at the Frankfurt fair with characteristic charm:

It has suddenly dawned on me, dear Paumgartner, that you do not always take care of yourself when you are away, often going to bed late and rising early, and I have provided you with only a traveling case [that is, with food sufficient only for the journey to Frankfurt]. Therefore, I have made you a little crackling. Now you may eat one when you first wake up and not have to fast so long.

Balthasar's brother-in-law Stephen Bair delivered the crackling; through kin, friends, and business couriers the two were constantly linked. Despite her disclaimer, Magdalena must have sent an exceedingly generous supply of crackling. Balthasar boasted that there was enough crackling for two fairs.

A devoted wife, Magdalena expected devotion in return. Tender expressions came less readily to Balthasar, but they did come. He always thought of her when eating good Italian melon in season. "I wish I could 'wish' some up to you," he writes, on one occasion offering his very own slice. When he learns she is ill, he has "all kinds of fearful thoughts," and he remains agitated until he learns from her or from another that her health has returned. Few letters from either fail at the outset to inquire if the other is "lively and well." Balthasar also occasionally surprised Magdalena with gifts of fabric and clothing, although his generosity was somewhat hampered by Magdalena's specific requests for so many items; a gift for her posed something of a test for Balthasar's imagination.

Balthasar was never, however, as regular a correspondent as Magdalena desired, and his failure to meet her expectations became a near-obsession with her. The correspondence we have contains five more letters from him than from her (eighty-seven to her eighty-two), but such statistics, even if they were complete, are a poor measure in matters of the heart. A particularly striking series of letters was exchanged on this subject in late 1591, when the couple had been married eight years and one might have expected delays in writing to be taken more in stride. Magdalena complains on December 1 that she has not heard from Balthasar for over two weeks (his last letter had been dated November 9) and accuses him of giving his business mail priority over writing to her. Reminding him of the joy his letters always bring her (and others), she begs that he not again make her wait more than two weeks.

Another week passes without a letter from Balthasar. An irritated Magdalena begins a new letter on December 9: "I cannot stop writing to you each week, even though you give me no reason to do so." Concerned that he may be ill, but just as worried that he may be growing indifferent to her, she assures him that she will become "quite dejected" should a letter not arrive by Saturday.

I cannot help thinking of the old proverb: "Out of sight, out of mind." Your brother tells me that you are preoccupied with a great many business letters, for which I think I am being made to suffer. . . . I pointedly reminded him that in the end I have simply to believe that there is no other reason for your not writing than that you have so much to do.

At the letter's end, Magdalena took a parting shot, but, characteristically, with more charm than fury. At a recent wedding party at the Pfinzings', she writes, many people asked her when she had last heard from Balthasar. Being too embarrassed to tell them that she had not heard from him for what would soon be a month, she was forced to lie: "I dissembled and said, 'Last week,' when it has already been three weeks! This for now!"

December 23, and Magdalena still has no letter from Balthasar. "Nonetheless," she writes, "I cannot stop writing to you each week, my heart's treasure, so long as we are apart. I hope to God we have survived the first half of our separation and that God will help us endure the next ten or eleven weeks until Lent," at which time Balthasar was scheduled to return from Lucca. She reports attending the engagement party of her brother Paul and Rosina Paumgartner, daughter of Burgomaster Hieronymus—a gala occasion, "completely stately," attended by a local count and countess. "I lacked for nothing except you!" she assures him, in a phrase she enjoyed repeating.

At last a letter from Balthasar, one unfortunately lost to us, written on December 4. Reassured by the letter, Magdalena eagerly seeks peace on the issue she now regrets having so keenly focused on. "I can well imagine," she now declares, "that you have a few more things to do than write letters to me. Therefore, you are excused." Balthasar, writing again from Lucca on Christmas Day, acknowledges receipt of her November letters and blames a business trip to Florence for his failure to write sooner. His frequent trips were his stock excuse, and a legitimate one. In his Christmas letter Balthasar makes no further comment on his tardy writing, but the letter is an unusual three manuscript pages long. On January 5, Balthasar receives Magdalena's letter of December 9, the most critical and sharply worded of all her letters. He characterizes it in his reply with the charged phrase "half angry." His own reaction is almost businesslike, even cold, as if he cannot for the life of him fathom Magdalena's distress over a letter or two. He thinks that she has simply let her emotions get the better of her out of fear that he has fallen seriously ill. The reader senses a man consumed by his work and irked by his wife's inability to take their relationship for granted. Balthasar may no longer be the romantic of their courtship days, but in his own eyes he remains the most diligent and dependable of mates, in whom the greatest confidence can be placed, a fact she of all people should know.

That I have not written to you for three weeks in a row is the result, first, of the fact that I have not had anything particularly letterworthy to write. Secondly, [regardless of] what Pfaud and others may imagine [about why I have not written to them], I do write to you every week when there is something to write about. Finally, I have not otherwise been neglectful of my work and business correspondence.

Why, Balthasar asks, after having learned from his brother Jörg that he was diligently writing his business letters every week, was she not satisfied? If he is alive, well, and gainfully employed, as Jörg has assured her, how can she be distressed? "Now, God willing, let this concern over the frequency of my writing end once and for all!"

A vain wish. In later years periods longer than three weeks would elapse between Balthasar's letters, and

Magdalena would again become "completely annoyed" with him. She even fretted over his reaction to the possible late arrival of her letters. Again we find Balthasar instructing her to suppress her "excessive, unnecessary worrying that I lay your letters to the side of my desk and give my other mail priority." The fact that the issue never died attests to the vitality of their love.

## ❧ SUBMISSION

MAGDALENA TO BALTHASAR
*19 April 1596, in Nuremberg*

Honest, kind, dear Paumgartner:
    Your pleasing letter reached me last Saturday through brother-in-law Jörg. I understand from it what I must get from Andreas Imhoff and Torisani. It will be done most diligently. I must also reserve with Torisani a barrel of wine [from a shipment] coming to him for the holidays; Hans Christoph Scheurl has also been promised one. However, he recently told brother-in-law Paul that if no one has need of it, he would allot it to him so we have the one we need for [Adam] Krämer, to whom I have already sent 2½ kegs.* Wilhelm Kress has taken 1½ kegs. I think the wine will have proved too expensive for Hans Christoph; it will come to 9 gulden before excise taxes. They say that one now may buy good wine at the marketplace for 5 gulden because, praise God, we have had the necessary good weather. Among the peasants at market Paul could get only 10½ to 11 gulden before excise taxes for last year's new wine. But he took it and distributed the wine.
    [Adam] Krämer this week sent us as a gift 2½-

* "2½ aeimer." *An Aeimer was ninety liters, and a barrel might contain up to four Aeimer.*

kegs of strong Egerich beer. He writes about how ill his wife is. He also wants you to write and let him know where the Franconian horsemen are mustering [for the Turkish front], if you can find out. He very much wants to know if they are returning to Eger. I thanked him for the beer; I must send him a Dutch cheese right away.

I am happy to hear that you are beginning your journey home so soon, on Tuesday, after the servant departs. May Almighty God give you luck and safety on your journey and help bring us together again in joy and health! Amen.

Hans Albrecht wrote to you this week, but as there was nothing pressing in the letter, I decided not to send it on to you. He writes mainly to say that we should undertake our planned trip as soon as possible. So I beg you most earnestly, dear Paumgartner, to let me know where around Fürth* you have in mind for us to meet you, and, depending on when you depart [Frankfurt] and when the springs [of Langenschwalbach] have refreshed you, about what time you should be arriving there. We very much want to come out and meet you with our two wagons full [of family and friends]. Just let me know from Frankfurt, or from wherever you can, so that we do not make the trip in vain.

If you see something that is rare and special when you are in Mainz or at the springs, please get it for me. Should you forget, I already have enough in you for which to give God thanks.

Brother-in-law Paul has wondered why you have not written a reply to his letter concerning the land purchase.†

Otherwise, I have nothing especially new to report, except that Hans Flenz is being buried today in the new *Bau*.‡ I was asked whether you might also join the funeral train. Yesterday Rosenthaler on Dieling Street died.

* *A few miles northwest of Nuremberg.*
† *A reference to an estate, Holenstein, that Balthasar was at this time attempting to buy.*
‡ *A quarter or ward of the city.*

Herewith is the newspaper from Herr König, who sends greetings. I went myself from vespers to fetch it from him. He says he is sorry he has not seen you for so long. I know nothing else to say to you, dear Paumgartner, except to ask that you take care of yourself. I do not know how you will be provided for in the kitchen. May it always be well with you! I have long wanted to hitch the three horses and, with brother-in-law Paul, come to you. But then I have thought better of it, [remembering that] you have not given me permission to do so, and it would also be expensive. And you have also said that you do not need me at this time. So I have restrained myself. Otherwise, I have devoted my week to cleaning and scrubbing.

Take my greetings into your heart of hearts, you chosen treasure, until God helps us come together again in joy. Brother-in-law Paul, Stephen Bair, his wife, and Christoph Behaim send sincere greetings. And Madela* says that I should greet Uncle warmly. She must be watching what I am doing, because there is nothing in your letter for her.

Be commended to Almighty God in grace,

*Magdalena Balthasar Paumgartner*

While Balthasar had traveled since his teens and knew the world beyond Nuremberg, Magdalena had seen little beyond the city's suburbs. That her horizons remained so restricted was not for lack of a desire to broaden them. She longed to join Balthasar for a holiday in Augsburg during one of his return trips from Italy. The very thought of such a rendezvous thrilled her. She writes of being "joyed by the prospect." The idea was less appealing to Balthasar, for whom Augsburg was just another all-too-familiar station on the

* *Magdalena's two-year-old niece, her brother Friedrich's youngest.*

merchant's busy circuit. Magdalena, however, persisted. Plans were first laid for such a meeting in the spring of 1592; however, a shattering family tragedy intervened.* In the summer of 1594, Magdalena again sought Balthasar's approval for an Augsburg meeting, this time during October. Her letters present him with a virtual fait accompli: brother-in-law Paul and brother Christoph have already volunteered to accompany her; brother Friedrich has agreed to provide a coach. She asks Balthasar for the exact date of his departure from Lucca so that she can time her arrival in Augsburg to coincide with his—she does not want to be there without him for more than two or three days. Where should they stay? The Lindemayr Inn, where Balthasar always goes, "but which will be very expensive," or would he prefer she try another place? She longs to see him and she clearly has romance on her mind: "My heart's treasure," she alleges in early August, "I won't know what to do with myself when I see and have you again. Our meeting seems so far away now; may God help us endure the two-month separation that still lies ahead."

Balthasar at this time was in the midst of a water cure for his chronic rheumatic pains and for an intestinal ailment, and he was thoroughly self-absorbed. He writes in mid-August, without so much as a mention of Augsburg, that he suspects it may be as late as All Saints Day, the very end of October, before he can depart Lucca. News of so late a departure shocked Magdalena, since it threw the trip well into November, when bad weather might cancel it. Was Balthasar being evasive? Henceforth, Magdalena's will was steeled.

She responded immediately that she had made plans to depart for Augsburg on October 11 or 12. Balthasar could well arrange his affairs to be there by October 15 or 16. Having assumed, possibly incorrectly, that he had already received her letter of July 10 in which she had

* See page 98.

specifically requested his agreement to the trip, she is understandably dismayed by his failure even to mention it. "I think you have forgotten about it," she humbly scolds. Then she informs him, with the subtlety of a freight wagon, that young Andreas Imhoff has given his wife permission to accompany her to Augsburg, even though she is pregnant. Dare Balthasar do less? If Balthasar had been contemplating continued resistance to the trip, Magdalena's final words must surely have given him pause. She assures him that, by her calculation, she will still have a good week to prepare for the trip if he will send his permission by return mail! "Friedrich Behaim's horse stands at the ready, dear Paumgartner."

Balthasar's next letter endorsed the plan. Despite the expense, Lindemayr's is the place to stay. He will send her an approximate date of his arrival in Augsburg before he departs Lucca. He insists that she make her travel arrangements through one Heinz Jörgen, apparently Balthasar's own travel agent or guide, and to forget the makeshift arrangements with her brothers and her brother-in-law Paul. Balthasar is emphatic that she not come if the weather turns bad—and not only because of the possible danger to her life and health. "If you travel in bad weather," he warns her, "you will be mocked; your trip will be interpreted as an act of folly!" He advises that she plan to bring along the goodly sum of one hundred gulden for expenses, as he will not be carrying much money on his person, a precaution against highwaymen and kidnappers on the route from Italy.

Balthasar's concluding comments on the Augsburg rendezvous cannot have pleased Magdalena. He was in an extremely bad mood, one of his frequent depressions brought on by the merchant schedule he had come to despise—this time exacerbated by the severity of his water cure, which had gone poorly, its tedium and expense outweighing any benefits. He speaks longingly of his departure from Italy as "my salvation from this land." In such a foul mood he closes his letter with the fond hope that he will not have to tarry long in Augsburg: "I do not look forward to spending even half a day there." A month later Balthasar projects the dates of his departure from Lucca and his arrival in Augsburg, adding his strongest caution yet: "I am still of the opinion that should the weather turn cold and the roads bad you should not come, simply because of the evil assassins [that is, highwaymen] and the gossip" it will occasion.

Magdalena's enthusiasm for the trip was not to be dimmed. Balthasar set a firm arrival date in Augsburg (October 25 or 26), but repeated his instructions to cancel the trip in the event of bad weather, seeming almost to be forecasting such. A charitable reader of Balthasar's letters, Magdalena was heartened by his grudging concurrence and attempted to shore up his weak resolve. "Because you nowhere in your letters indicate that you have said anything about this trip to anyone else, I wonder if you are truly serious about it," she gently scolds. She is "completely terrified" by his estimate of the expense (100 gulden) and assures him she can do much better. According to her brother Christoph, the cost can be kept between 50 and 60 gulden if, as she intends, they stick to her original, family-assisted travel plans. This would mean free transportation under the care and protection of Christoph and Paul Paumgartner, who, she reports, vouch for the horse, and whose expertise as guides she obviously esteems more highly than does Balthasar.

Did the trip take place? Possibly, although no records directly confirm it. Was it all that Magdalena had hoped it would be? Probably. Two years later she expressed a longing to hitch the horses and join Balthasar in Frankfurt, and on this occasion she was clearly rebuffed. She would not have wanted to join him, however, had un-

*Balthasar is depicted on a medallion commemorating his death. (See p. 25.)*
Reprinted by permission of the Germanisches Nationalmuseum.

pleasantness been her only expectation, and she did regularly ride out to intercept him in celebratory fashion with family and friends at towns within a few miles of home, on those occasions when he provided advance information of his arrival time. In April 1596, Magdalena is firmly denied a rendezvous. She is nonetheless as disarming as ever, playing the submissive wife and cutting her losses. In one line of her letter of April 19 she begs Balthasar to keep an eye out for an unusual gift for her as he swings down through Mainz to the baths of Langenschwalbach; in the next she expresses fulfillment and contentment in having him alone. In one breath she brags about her wifely obedience; in the next she pointedly reminds him of his professed ability, on this occasion, to manage without her. She worries about how well he is cared for in the kitchen, while at the same time portraying herself, alone and barely remembered, a housekeeping drudge. It is a letter designed to win a husband's submission.

# III

# PARTNERS

Balthasar, like his contemporaries, had a relatively narrow choice of occupation. Since generations of men on both sides of his family had been merchants, as a boy he was destined for the merchant's life. Apprenticeship began between the ages of twelve and fifteen, after a boy had learned to read, write, and calculate skillfully. Balthasar may also have attended Latin school as his son later did. The apprenticeship customarily lasted five to seven years, but could be much longer, and the young apprentices went abroad for at least a part of their time, because a knowledge of foreign languages and customs was essential to success.

Physical endurance was a major asset, as merchants traveled regularly between sources and markets; the semiannual Nuremberg merchants' convoy to Frankfurt was a week's journey. Having a way with words also helped: it gave a merchant an edge in the haggling and bill-collecting that were a routine part of his life. Success often depended on knowledge and skills that only long experience could convey, especially, an ability to anticipate demand, spot bargain quality goods, and develop a network of trustworthy contacts and assistants strategically placed between sources and markets.

## BALTHASAR TO HIS FATHER
*7 May 1572, in Nuremberg*

Filial love and devotion to you, dear father. Your letter of [May] 6 has happily arrived. I think that you have, however, forgotten to send the cloak for Helena.* She would still like for you to do so at the first opportunity, because she needs it.

I have not lately forgotten to enclose the letter concerning Sebald Bucher. I have just been unable to get it from Uncle. He told me a few days ago that he was going to give me the letter. But the other day after he wrote it, he was out of the office and I could not find it. I am sending it to you now with this letter.

Master Jörg began to patch the roof on your house the day before yesterday. I think he should be done with it today. I will pay him according to your instruction; I can also delay payment until you come here yourself, as I understand little about such work. So far I have not paid him anything.

Schmidmaier has again paid Uncle 30 gulden on behalf of Martin Pfinzing's heirs for a half year's use of 1,000 gulden. He says he once recorded [the name] Balthasar Paumgartner, so he knows no one else but you with that name. He also paid 6 gulden more on the past-due interest. Hieronymus Schnitter paid 25 gulden and Sigmund Haller 12.10. Together with the 50 from Bucher, it comes to a total of 123.10. I have handed all of it over to Uncle Albrecht Scheurl, who would like to have instruction from you on its disposition. If you desire, I will use some of it to buy a small barrel of freshly tapped wine for Hans at the Heilbronner Inn. If you want the remainder in small coins, tell me whether three-kreuzer pieces will be serviceable, perhaps a mixture of royal Bohemian and Swiss. I would like to see if I can make a 100 percent profit on an exchange for such coins. This week a district conference [on currency] is being held here attended by many foreign people. I believe what good it accomplishes will

* *Balthasar's sister.*

mostly affect coinage. Swiss coins are now plummeting and talers are forcibly declining. Among the few one can still find, half are Swiss. We will soon be wanting a sum of talers for several lords in Augsburg. In order to get them more easily, they are permitting us to pay a half percent a hundred in exchange rates against other gross coinage; in Augsburg, they are paying a half to two-thirds percent. Where it [will] stop [is not yet clear]; may it continue as it is going!

Uncle Albrecht Scheurl asks that you remember the agreement with him and send his [share].

I have happily learned that you will be traveling here soon; since then Uncle Albrecht Scheurl told me to make ready. When Wilhelm returns, they are planning to send me to Lucca. But how and under what circumstances and in what capacity I will be going, I have not the slightest indication. I learned about these plans from Herr Nützel, who thinks I should ask Uncle exactly what they have in mind for me, so that I may know how I am going to live there. Simply to move there would be little help to me. Herr Nützel is certainly right; but, as always, I do not like to confront Uncle with these questions; I worry—indeed, I know for an absolute certainty—that he would not take it kindly. Thus is it ever my misfortune that I alone do not permit myself to act—this time stuck here and so completely useless. Yesterday Uncle was asked whether he thought I might be in Lucca for a long time. He indicated to me that they had not yet discussed it, and that they would not decide until after the fall fair at the earliest. I can safely conclude from this that they have no desire to do anything with me at this time. For this reason, he wants you to come here that much sooner.

Otherwise nothing more; may God keep you.

*Balthasar Paumgartner the Younger*

# ❖MURDER ROAD

When Balthasar wrote this letter to his father in Altdorf, he was twenty-one years of age and at the end of
an apprenticeship in Nuremberg, apparently with his
uncle Albrecht Scheurl. Apart from the family business,
he is preoccupied with a rumor that he is soon to be
sent to Lucca, Italian base for many Nuremberg merchant firms. The prospect of such an assignment pleases
and excites him, but the uncertainty and vagueness of
the rumor also deeply trouble him. How will he go,
where will he lodge, what position will he hold, what
will his duties be? Unfortunately, he lacks the courage
to approach his uncle for more information, believing
firmly that such questions would be mistaken as cheeky.
The more recent discovery that no firm decision on his
departure will be made until after the fall fair, a good
six months away, has left him dejected and self-accusing.
He hopes that his father, who plans soon to come to
Nuremberg, may be able to assist, at least gain more
information. Meanwhile, Balthasar is "stuck" in Nuremberg and "completely useless."

By 1582, when the correspondence with Magdalena
commences, Balthasar is an independent merchant and
a seasoned traveler between Nuremberg, Lucca, and
Frankfurt. From his base in Lucca he gathers merchandise from throughout north-central Italy, which he then
ships to customers in Nuremberg and at the Frankfurt
spring and fall fairs. He is betrothed and will soon
marry. Still, the anxious youth of 1572 continues to
live in the experienced man of 1582. More than ever he
believes himself to be at the mercy of forces beyond his
control. He is cautious to the point of indecision, full of
complaints, hopeful that someone, God or man, will intervene and provide relief. The apprentice languishing

in Nuremberg is now a vexed merchant in Lucca. His old Aunt Scheurl, to whom he felt particularly close, shares with Magdalena—with whom she has become good friends—a letter in which he confides his boredom and constant worry. Magdalena offers quick and profuse consolation to her unhappy fiancé ("Would to God that I could help you bear this worry," she writes), but she seems also to have been pleased by his boredom, which she takes as a sign that she is missed and needed. However, Balthasar's letter complaining that his only amusement had been a troop of visiting players who had among them an "indescribably eloquent and skillful" woman, and his raving about her at length, may have stimulated feelings of jealousy on her part.

With the passage of years, Balthasar felt increasingly besieged by his work, and complaints about boredom, worry, and insecurity become more frequent. In July 1584 he writes to Magdalena from Lucca, exhausted by his work, depressed by seemingly endless conflict with his elder brother Caspar with whom he competed for his father's favor, and also mourning the recent death of a friend in Nuremberg.

I know nothing of happiness. Whether I am at the springs or here, there is joy all around me, while I am quiet and sad and often I may say nothing at all. I am my own enemy and thus may grumble. Many who know me well frequently complain about how I have never in my life talked a lot. My greatest joy here comes on Sunday evening with the mail; I always look forward to it with great longing. Thank God, each day a day passes.

He finds Frankfurt just as inhospitable as Italy, "a purgatory" from which he worries he may someday be unable to extricate himself. In the spring of 1586, he writes that he has had his fill of Frankfurt, "as if I had eaten it with a spoon," and he confides to Magdalena his fear that one day or the next will prove to be his complete ruin there. On another occasion we find him counting the hours as he waits to depart Frankfurt with the merchants' convoy, demoralized by the delay, his dependence on the convoy, and the prospect of traveling with an ailing horse he has been unable to sell. "Things never go as I think they will," he confesses. "I must surrender myself to the fact that nothing ever happens according to my will as I have planned it."

Balthasar's letters are a running commentary on the dark side of the merchant's trade. He is haunted by physical danger along the merchant routes that he and his colleagues call "Murder Road." In March 1591, he writes to Magdalena from Frankfurt greatly relieved after a threatening but safe journey there.

Early last Tuesday, after I had written you a brief letter, I suddenly fell despondent, as if a fever were descending upon me. Thereafter the entire journey took a turn for the worse. But, praise and thank God, I have since become much better and I am enjoying food and drink again. Since then my brother Jörg, praise God, has also safely arrived with the convoy and our wares. So far no one who has arrived has been intercepted by foreign soldiers on the terrible, murderous road that leads here from everywhere.

The merchants monitor reports of highwaymen as diligently as they do reports of the weather. When highwaymen pose no threat, soldiers or mercenaries of one faction or another may cut the trade routes just as effectively. Beset by neither highwaymen nor soldiers, the merchants may encounter townspeople who, suspicious and fearful of strangers who might be bearing plague, suddenly close their gates to all travelers. The safe transit of Italian goods north to Nuremberg and Frankfurt is never assured.

The seasons play havoc with the merchants' health. Balthasar's hands are swollen and cracked after weeks on horseback in wintry weather. His sinuses and lungs

*A view of Nuremberg, a safe haven in a forbidding world, and its surrounding woods, from 1516.*
Reprinted by permission of the Germanisches Nationalmuseum, Nuremberg.

fill so with mucus from colds and flu that he runs out
of handkerchiefs. Summer heat waves stop all travel in
its tracks, and famines strike year round, lining the merchant routes with "faces of pitiably wretched common
folk."

The physical hazards alone did not alienate Balthasar
from his work. He would not have liked his job under
ideal physical conditions. Balthasar lacked the stomach
for the essential tasks of the merchant's trade—bargaining over prices and collecting receipts. He loathed
competition and confrontation. When, in the fall of
1584, his departure for home from the Frankfurt fair
was delayed, it was because "money runs hot and sour"
from the hands of his customers—they were paying up,
but angrily and reluctantly, and he lacked the will to
pursue them. Back at the fair the following spring, he
frankly admits his failings. "I am now involved in the
most arduous work. For my part, I wish it were over and
done with; then something good would gladly be due
me. But for now I must demand payments. Plenty of
screaming and bickering will be the result, and for this
reason I would much prefer to be at home." In 1592, he
left his "most difficult ever" Frankfurt spring fair prematurely, as soon as negotiations were set in place, turn-
ing matters over to surrogates and subordinates. The
following fall the "torment and vexation of the fair"
whipped him again. "The longer I remain in Frankfurt,
the more I suffer," he tells Magdalena. He contrasts his
"bare ability to tolerate the petty demands of the marketplace" with the greater patience and skill of cousin
Paul Scheurl. When the 1593 spring fair concluded, he
informed Magdalena that whereas the arduous work of
buying and selling had ended, the other and even more
difficult work of the fair still lay ahead, namely, "the
exchange of money, and with it much screaming and
bickering, and also cursing." Ten days later he rejoiced
that the haggling had stopped. He planned to depart
"soon, and happily" if one unfinished piece of business

could be quickly concluded; he hastened, however, to add, with characteristic caution bred of many disappointments, "but what one would like, one cannot always have."

The fall of 1596 brought a new aggravation. The Imperial Coinage Commission, under the co-chairmanship of Count Georg von Erbach and a Bamberg physician, Dr. Achaz Hüls, the immediate authority, began to implement new, unfavorable exchange rates at the fair. The result was for Balthasar a "bad, unprofitable, unhappy, confused, and factious fair. . . . May the Lord God forgive this man [Dr. Hüls] for breaking so many hearts. The regulation of currency is not a job for a physician alone; the counsel of practical and knowledgeable businessmen should also have been heard." Dr. Hüls continued to cause "all kinds of hindrances, disorder, harm, and ill will" at the 1597 fair, but an incapacitating ear infection gave Balthasar something else to fret over. For his health's sake, Balthasar confined himself to quarters, staying inside and keeping warm, retiring early with a bowl of soup and two eggs, his head tightly wrapped in an old shirt. This double dose of bad luck, illness on top of financial loss, brings back a favorite expression of exasperation: "I have had my fill of Frankfurt, as if I had eaten it with a spoon."

Family troubles also pursued Balthasar to Lucca and Frankfurt, especially the rivalry with his scoundrel older brother Caspar. He and Magdalena believed that whenever Balthasar was out of town Caspar seized the opportunity to plot against them. Almost a month to the day before Balthasar and Magdalena's wedding, Magdalena learned that Caspar was trying to move his own marriage celebration—his second—to the week immediately preceding theirs. She angrily reported this brazen attempt to "crowd us out," fearing that no game would be left over for their own wedding feast should Caspar succeed. (He apparently did not.) A year later, Magdalena and Paul Scheurl reported more "shabby deal-

*A view of Frankfurt at sunrise in 1646 by Matthais Merian.*
*The wine market is prominent in the left foreground.*
From *Topographia Hassiae . . . durch Matthais Merian* (Frankfurt a.M., 1655; photo-reprint edition, 1959). Reprinted by permission of Johannes Stauda Verlag, Kassel.

ings" by Caspar, which this time included slandering Balthasar to his father. Balthasar wrote directly to Caspar for an explanation, which proved neither clarifying nor satisfying. He attempted to be prudent and philosophical about his brother by "neither ignoring nor exaggerating" his scheming. But the emotional toll that Caspar's efforts to alienate him from their father took on Balthasar is indicated by his reaction to news of the deaths of friends in Nuremberg: "Would to God that I had been sent such news of my filthy brother, with whose dirty dealings we all must contend!"

Magdalena also felt emotionally besieged by Caspar. In the summer of 1584, Caspar's wife had been fined twenty gulden for her role in the punishment of a servant accused of stealing; the servant, caught in the act, had been imprisoned and flogged without a proper hearing. As it turned out, the servant claimed to have "stolen at her master's instruction," and on these grounds she successfully appealed her punishment to the burgomaster. Given the circumstances of the servant's relationship with Caspar and his wife, her act was deemed malicious rather than criminal and their silent complicity punishable by fine. "He is no brother to you, that foul man!" Magdalena scoffs. A few months later Caspar's wife appeared before the Five, a tribunal of councilmen who adjudicated petty crimes and injuries, to answer charges that she had struck her servant with a stick of wood. "Would that the girl had struck her back!" Magdalena wishes. The hostility persisted. In her January 1592 report to Balthasar of recent deaths and burials in Nuremberg, Magdalena included one Rafael Behaim, an apparent criminal who had died in prison, and one with whom Balthasar had earlier had conflict. Commenting on his procession to the grave, Magdalena could not suppress the wish "Had Caspar only accompanied him!"

In the end, Balthasar survived the fraternal challenge,

both emotionally and in fact. In November 1591, Caspar, alleging dire need, had persuaded his father to lend him fifteen gulden to buy a suit of clothes for the coming winter. As Magdalena was an expert judge of quality materials and workmanship, Herr Paumgartner asked Balthasar's brother Jörg to have her examine Caspar's selection and assure him that the money was being well spent. (Caspar must at this time have been a man in his early forties and enormously undisciplined.) Magdalena was cynical about the whole undertaking. "If he wears it to the next public house [he visits] and loses it," she snaps, "then the next time we must dress him in a stone suit." Two days after the suit had been purchased on Magdalena's recommendation, she found it right back on the merchant's rack in the marketplace. According to the salesperson, Caspar had returned it and gotten a refund, alleging the suit to be an improper fit. Magdalena suspected that the salesperson had also been in on the scam, getting a kickback from Caspar for agreeing to take the suit back, while still being able to resell the suit at full price. Attempts by Jörg to retrieve the money proved futile. Only six gulden remained when he caught up with Caspar. Balthasar expressed disgust with Caspar's "dog behavior," but he now felt confident that his father had seen so many examples of it that this latest display would not unduly upset him. Balthasar declined to become directly involved, although he did write to Burgomaster Hieronymus Paumgartner and Paul Scheurl to ask them to assist his father. "Caspar will not improve," Magdalena concluded of the affair, "until he is put into jail."

Three years later Caspar did land in prison, for swindling a local countess. He had taken payment of seventy-two gulden from her for some goods he never delivered. Both Caspar and his wife begged members of the family to reimburse the Count, the key condition of Caspar's early release, his wife going so far as to warn that Caspar would commit suicide if left long in prison. All refused to intervene, however, and none more firmly nor with a greater sense of rectitude than Balthasar.

A suspicion of resentment and ill will toward him on the part of others, at times approaching paranoia, was a fixed part of Balthasar's emotional world. The physical vulnerability, competition, and uncertain fortunes of the merchant's life explain much of it, but persistent family strife also played a role in creating his state of mind. Balthasar bared his soul to Magdalena in 1596 after a depressing encounter with a new brother-in-law, Alexander Geuder, a powerful aristocrat whose family had two representatives (the legal limit) among the city's powerful thirteen senior burgomasters. Balthasar was then trying to buy land in the Upper Palatinate from the domain of the Count of Ortenburg and thereby move up into the more settled life of a country gentleman. Closing the deal had proved difficult because the laws governing such purchases were complex and strongly favorable to the nobility in negotiations. Balthasar shared his plans and frustrations with his sister Susanna and Geuder, who had married the previous year. Geuder, however, resented his projected move from Nuremberg and appears to have sneered at his aristocratic ambitions, preferring, Balthasar believed, to see him confined to a small merchant's life in the city. Balthasar writes to Magdalena about the encounter.

Brother-in-law Alexander Geuder has been here today with his wife. I noticed under the surface that a passionate envier had also come along in him, one who purposefully wanted to sour my life. He wished me much luck, but behind his words he thought otherwise. He talked about how an official had said that those burghers who want to take what is theirs and leave their present residence in the city and set themselves up on such landed estates, thereby completely renouncing their citizenship, should be bidden to take their penny and go! Indeed, one overcomes many things by patience, and treachery usually slays its own masters.

Balthasar did manage to acquire an estate, Holenstein, in the Upper Palatinate. That he could accomplish this is a commentary on the success of his business; that it was a financial strain shows that he had accumulated no fortune. He complains to Magdalena in September that it will cause him "no small disturbance and harm" to pay for Holenstein at the new devalued currency rates. After March 1597, Balthasar settled into his estate for the remaining three years of his life, no longer a prisoner of the dreaded semiannual fairs.

As difficult as he found the merchant's life, and as much as he had come to dislike it, Balthasar also considered it a blessing. It had given him order and discipline without which he feared he might have become indolent and alcoholic. Balthasar makes his most constructive comments on the life of a merchant in this context: he admits to a proclivity to drink excessively, especially on festive occasions, and he believes it is his work that has enabled him to control it. When in 1592 Magdalena describes the Christmas festivities she believes he is unhappily missing, Balthasar is delighted to learn of the fun she is having, but he also expresses relief that his work has kept him away from the temptations that accompany such celebrations.

I am glad that so much good spirit, entertaining of guests, and feasting—a veritable fool's paradise—exists in the world around you. But I am even more pleased that my work prevents me from being part of it. I am thereby spared much excessive and harmful drinking. Believe me, I am much healthier in my regimen here.

According to William Smith, Nuremberg's reputation as a city in which every man "shall be sometimes overseen in drink" was quite undeserved; he had rather found Nuremberg, unlike the towns of Saxony, to be a place where a man's refusal to drink was respected. Clearly for Balthasar the temptation on festive occasions was too great and his will too weak. He admonishes Magdalena that it is "no act of friendship" on her part when she wishes he were present with her at feasts and banquets. "Here, in my sober, ordered business life, I am and will remain much healthier." Nevertheless Magdalena could not suppress a wish to have him by her side at yet another feast. "I lacked for nothing except you," she tells him as she reports her fun. But then she quickly adds: "However, I completely agree with you that, as you write, it is much better that you are not here, because of the immoderate drinking."

# ❩ STROKING THE TAIL OF THE FOX

MAGDALENA TO BALTHASAR
*18 April 1594, in Nuremberg*

Honest, kind, dear Paumgartner:
Your letter from Augsburg has come. I will hope in Almighty God that when this letter reaches [Lucca], you will also, with God's help, already have arrived there. May he again grant you his divine grace!
I am happy to learn that the horses [you are planning to buy] have been well cared for up to now.
I paid the tailor already after your departure, but he tells me there is no woolen material left over.
When [our servant] Hans arrives, I will send him also to the count, as you instruct.
I have given your brother Jörg the money that belongs to Bartel Albrecht to deliver to him. Brother-in-law Jörg tells me that someone has already written to you about your estimated payments in Frankfurt.
I will not neglect to admonish the peasants [in

Wöhrd], and I will see that brother-in-law Paul does so in Engelthal.

The wine, or rather new wine, came the Sunday after your departure. Brother-in-law Jörg has calculated the cost at 23 gulden per large measure, no less. I have sent one to [your] father, to Wilhelm Imhoff, and to Wilhelm Kress. Since [Paul] Behaim did not want one, Kress asked me to let him have it. So I have laid aside only one for ourselves. One for [Wolf] Rehlein; the Pfauds one. When I get the bill for the excise tax, which Jörg calculated for me on each measure, I will send each one a bill for his share.

Otherwise the matter is settled. I did, however, have a fight with the wine controller. When I sent him the money, 34 gulden, he sent it back to me, tore up the original bill, and said he had to make a new one because an additional barrel bought at the market must be added. I twice sent word to him that I knew of no such purchase and that you bought no wine whatsoever at the market, otherwise one would know about it. Finally, brother-in-law Jörg went there, returned, and asked if perhaps Hans had taken a barrel on your behalf, and it then dawned on me for the first time that the barrel we had drunk so quickly you had gotten with Hans. So I had to send him 40¾ gulden. He informed me that it had been a good nine weeks since he had given you the bill for that barrel. I am puzzled why you have been so slow to pay it.

Kind, dear treasure, I have nothing more to write at this time, except that the delivery of invitations* [to brother Paul's wedding] has gone well, four happy tables [of guests have promised to come]. May God grant that the wedding also goes well.

* Heimladung. *William Smith describes this custom: "Six days before the marriage, they write up the names of all those which they will have bidden to the wedding and deliver the same to one, whose office is to bid to weddings and burials (whereof there is about 12 in all). This man goes in stately manner with another, noting all them that promise to come, till he has his just number, for above 60 may not come to supper (which is 5 tables and 12 at every table)."*

Friendly and warm greetings to you, dearest treasure; may God keep you in his grace.

*Magdalena Balthasar Paumgartner*

When Balthasar was on the road, Magdalena became his Nuremberg distributor, bookkeeper, and collection agency. She began to assume such responsibilities before their marriage, as if they were part of the wedding preparations. Balthasar writes her from Lucca in December 1582 with instructions to inform Frau Lochner that he has ordered the crimson satin lining she desired and the bicolored double taffeta. He ships to Magdalena five barrels of wine, three of which she is instructed to send on to his father in Altdorf, while laying aside the two best for their wedding day. Magdalena received these goods, paid the delivery fees and tariffs required by the city, and carefully maintained the receipts.

Over the years such responsibilities grew into a virtual partnership. In addition to regular shipments of Miltenberg wine, she received and disbursed to their Nuremberg clients and relatives a great variety of merchandise. The standard cloth items from Italy were linen and damask, but expensive velvet often arrived. Magdalena sometimes kept the best pieces for herself. When regular shipments of flax arrived, she carefully inspected them for signs of damage, as flax did not travel well. Winestocks and grains were also regular items. Then there were Milanese Parmesan and Dutch cheeses; a large whole salmon (seventeen pounds, parceled out to customers piece by piece); seeds, including pumpkin (for which Balthasar sent precise planting instructions); and artichokes, which Magdalena started indoors in pots while the weather was still cold. Magdalena's favorite personal orders were Würzburg quinces, pears, and nuts, for which she regularly reminds Balthasar to keep his eyes open. In one shipment, he sends the following items, which suggest the range of his shopping list: forty-nine pounds of Dutch cheeses (for Andreas Imhoff); seven pairs of shoes and two pairs of slippers; a German Bible (for Hans Christoph Scheurl); two Jacobus Francus newspapers (popular semiannual reports written specifically for the fairs, one with an engraving for Paul Scheurl); and other newspapers (mostly for Balthasar's own enjoyment); and Cambrai flax. All such goods normally arrived in numbered crates, Balthasar sending crate numbers and brief descriptions of the merchandise ahead to Magdalena so that, knowing well in advance what to expect, she might prepare for storage and distribution.

Among Magdalena's more exacting chores was the billing of peasant customers and clients, to whom they sold cheap knives and wine and from some of whom they also collected rents. On one occasion Balthasar urged Magdalena to seek the assistance of his brothers Jörg and Paul to collect delinquent peasant debts, warning that "if the peasants do not pay in full this year, they never will." Magdalena's acts and agenda for the week surrounding April 18, 1594, give us an idea of the range of things that could occupy the attention and time of a merchant's wife. She had paid the tailor; was making plans to receive and instruct a servant; was taking steps to admonish peasants in Wöhrd to pay their bills and to prod her brother-in-law to do the same with peasant customers in Engelthal; had given money to her brother-in-law to deliver to a creditor; had discussed Balthasar's anticipated expenses at the Frankfurt fair; had received and distributed a shipment of wine; was preparing to bill each recipient for his fair share of the excise tax; had quarreled with the wine controller and researched his additional charge before paying the wine tax; and, finally, was continuing to assist with the preparations for her brother's wedding.

Balthasar frequently admonished Magdalena to keep exact records. On one occasion he suggests she ask cousin Paul Scheurl for help if her calculations become too difficult, an indication of the magnitude of her tasks. Magdalena's letters regularly provide accountings of her disbursements. In April 1593 we find a receipt detailing the distribution of a wagonload of wine. The item is particularly interesting because it acknowledges an unsuspected occupational hazard of a merchant's wife. As was customary, she had snatched out for themselves what seemed to be the best of the barrels. However, before she could determine this, it had been necessary for her to taste each barrel, as new wine and inferior afterwine had been mixed together in the shipment. She confesses to "having almost gotten drunk" in the line of duty.

In addition to her mercantile responsibilities, Magdalena had to cope with the many problems of home ownership. Between 1587 and 1589 she completely refurbished their house, directing the work of potters, carpenters, plasterers, and glaziers. Among the problems she had to deal with were snails in the walls—the result of a privy that had been "misplaced" by Balthasar, so that it drew moisture and snails from a pond nearby. She also had the unpleasant task of disciplining a rude, destructive, and drunken servant, whom, with the assistance of Paul Scheurl, she first fired, then rehired on condition of good behavior pending Balthasar's return.

Magdalena's shrewdness as a businesswoman was a trait Balthasar had perceived early in their relationship. During their engagement he praised her skill in gaining the friendship of his Aunt Scheurl, of whom he was outspokenly fond. For family reasons, Balthasar was eager to maintain the old lady's goodwill (she happened to be wealthy and influential), so he encouraged Magdalena to deepen their relationship by confiding in her and seeking her advice, which he knew from experience would please his aunt. "But you already know well how to stroke the tail of the fox," he tells Magdalena, certainly high praise from a merchant.

No small part of Magdalena's responsibilities at home

involved these acts of diplomacy and goodwill, a role she self-consciously played and entirely relished. At a wedding party at the home of Frau Carl Pfinzing she is "standing in" for Balthasar and "playing the toady." She tells Balthasar she blessed this second marriage of Siegfried Pfinzing "in your place." Enjoying her role as the merchant's wife, she is an innovative and charming businesswoman. She sends a note to old Frau Köppel in Schlackenwalde (apparently the wife of the merchant Hans Köppel, who supplied Balthasar with rabbits and chickens when he took the waters at nearby Carlsbad), to remind her not to forget to send flax; as a special reminder she sends along a dozen honey cakes (*Lebkuchen*). When five melons arrive as a gift from the "secretary of Bamberg," she promptly sends a note of thanks to him on Balthasar's behalf. On one occasion she reports sending a gilded silver toothpick suspended from three small chains—a novelty that had caught her eye while she was shopping in the marketplace—to Hans Albrecht, Balthasar's distant older brother, a silversmith who lived in Vienna, with whom Balthasar negotiated shares of the family inheritance after their father's death; the toothpick was to be a gift for his son. Balthasar reacted with pleasure to news that the Duchess of Pomersfelden, "without special prodding," had sent Magdalena thirty gulden, another indication that Magdalena regularly billed their customers and expertly maintained the accounts. Balthasar trusted Magdalena with his most sensitive papers. In the spring of 1587 he instructs her to be ready to take the last will and testament of one Eberhard Khürn from his "iron money box" and present it to Khürn's brother and nephew in the event of Khürn's death.

Balthasar respected and regularly sought Magdalena's business judgment. On one occasion he describes a bed curtain bought and sent ahead to her, adding that if it does not please her or she believes it to be too expensive she should have the dealer resell it for the best price it can fetch. In September 1592, he solicits her reaction to the possible sale of his two brown horses to an agent of the Bishop of Salzburg at the Frankfurt fair. He contemplates buying two young "beautiful grays" if two of the same color and size turn up at the fair. But he hesitates, he says, because he would prefer to face the summer rather than the winter with two new horses. Magdalena advises against buying the grays if the deal for the browns is not firm. Apart from the expense of maintaining two additional horses, she warns, "Should you bring the four horses together, a buyer may want to pay you less for the two browns. But it is your decision to make, and what pleases you also pleases me." On occasion Magdalena directly criticizes Balthasar's business judgment. Once he sent her some curtain material which she considered a bad buy ("the wrong color and not fit for hanging"). She sent it back to him to resell in Frankfurt to avoid the loss they would take on it if she sold it in Nuremberg. With mild exasperation she points out that had he first consulted her, the error would have been prevented.

Magdalena's skill in personal and family matters was as impressive as her business judgment. During a season of plague in Nuremberg in 1585, she made plans to move with their son, little Balthasar, at the time a toddler, to neighboring Altdorf for safety. Andreas Imhoff asked her to take along his two young children, Jörg and Marina, because his wife refused to go with the children and leave him alone in Nuremberg. This created difficulty for Magdalena. She had little Balthasar to look after, and her lodgings in Altdorf were modest and could not readily accommodate two additional children, especially one as "active" as Jörg, who was nine or ten. Not wishing to refuse their friends in time of need, but also not wanting to make her own life unmanageable, Magdalena negotiated through her new brother-in-law, Wilhelm Kress, to take only Marina, for whom a pallet could easily be laid in the maid's room. Jörg she feared would "be always out the door." Learning of her solution, Balthasar praised her handling of the matter "so diplomatically."

On another occasion, Magdalena solicited Balthasar's help in smoothing the marriage negotiations between her brother Paul and Hieronymus Paumgartner's daughter Rosina. Magdalena believed it an ideal union. She describes Rosina as "right for Paul, large and strong, just what he needs." However, Herr Paumgartner (then perhaps the city's most powerful man), while personally pleased with Paul, sought greater detail about his finances. Balthasar's brother Paul also became involved in the discussions, contributing information about their branch of the Paumgartner tree. Magdalena asked Balthasar to write Herr Paumgartner a "friendly letter" and "not forget to talk about property." She also thought it would be a good idea for him to send greetings to Herr Paumgartner's new son-in-law, Joachim Kleewein, who had just married the younger Paumgartner daughter Clara, and wish him good luck.

The passage of Archbishop Wolfgang of Mainz, an electoral prince of the Empire, through Nuremberg in 1594 with a train of six hundred horsemen en route to the Imperial Diet gave Magdalena still another opportunity to exhibit her diplomatic skills. Her brother Paul, along with other city officials, had extended customary hospitality to the Archbishop's party as visiting political dignitaries. Magdalena's house had initially been volunteered as one of the party's lodgings, but she, appalled at the notion of quartering strangers in her home while Balthasar was away, sought an exemption on grounds that she had "no man in the house." She relays to Balthasar her great relief at gaining the exemption and describes with mild shock the arrival of the Archbishop at the home of Hans Welser "with 242 horsemen." Her success also pleased Balthasar, who by this time rather expected it.

Magdalena participated in the cultural life of Nurem-

berg and knew what was going on in the larger political
world outside the city. Her interests and activities extended well beyond the chores of family and business.
She keeps Balthasar abreast of local events: fires in the
city, the execution of a fruit dealer and a specialty weaver
for sodomy, even a trout-fishing expedition, the details
of which she learned from Jakob Imhoff. The deaths of
friends, acquaintances, even strangers, are so dutifully
reported that a virtual obituary section appears in most
of her letters. She conveys the latest news about the
Strasbourg Bishop's War (1592–93), including casualty
figures and the number of enemy flags (three) captured
by the Protestant leader, Duke Christian of Anhalt. Between 1592 and 1594, her letters carry the highlights of
western Europe's war against the Turks in Hungary, as
Nuremberg became a staging area for troops en route to
the front.

Magdalena also occasionally hobnobbed with elite intellectuals and politicians, and she did not spare them
criticism. Attending founder's day at the Altdorf Academy, she witnessed the installation of the locally famous
scholar Johann Praetorius as rector, an event she found
so boring that she promised to stay home with Balthasar
on the next founder's day. When she dined with a count
in Altdorf after a wedding party, apparently for the
Count's cook, she did not relish the meal. "They had
many courses," she informs Balthasar, "but little to eat,
as the food was so God-awfully prepared in their Polish
manner."

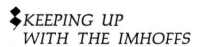

## ❖ KEEPING UP
## WITH THE IMHOFFS

MAGDALENA TO BALTHASAR
*9 December 1591, in Nuremberg*

Honest, friendly, dear Paumgartner:
I cannot stop writing to you every week, even though

you give me no reason to do so. It is now three weeks since I last heard from you and there may be no letter again this Saturday, which will leave me quite dejected. I cannot help thinking of the old proverb: "Out of sight, out of mind." Your brother tells me that you are preoccupied with a great many business letters, for which I think I am being made to suffer. Your not writing has made me wonder whether you are well, but Jörg gives me to understand that you are doing a great deal of writing. I pointedly reminded him that in the end I have simply to believe that there is no other reason for your not writing to me than that you have so much to do. He says that he understands from your letter [to him] that you will be departing Lucca before the fair. Confirmation of this I eagerly await with all my heart in your letter on Saturday; such news from you also makes me happy. We are, praise and thank God, still as we were, in good health; may God continue to keep us both so. Amen.

Dear Paumgartner, I am writing this letter because of the boy, who constantly admonishes me when I write to ask you to bring him a suit of clothes. So I am sending along with this letter a measure of the length and width of the jacket, also the length of the sleeves and the pants, all of which I have taken liberally from his old velvet suit, which still fits him properly, and I have also measured him. Choose only something black, for he already has two colored suits. Of course, in this matter it is yours to do as you please.

Old Bair is the same as a week ago; one still believes he cannot last more than three or four days. Every day some rotted flesh is cut away from his wound. However, he feels no pain and he no longer asks for anyone. He speaks only when he is thirsty or wants something to eat. He has lost interest in everything. May the Lord God end it soon for him.

Frau Tobias Kastner sends warm greetings to you. She is now living here with her mother on the third floor of Frau Lienhart Grundherr's house. She had traveled around for three days with her mother before arriving. Blood has begun to flow from her mouth, and she is so weak that I do not know if she will last long. I visit her often, for she was earlier going to put up with us. She has now been sick here for three weeks. I worry that she will not last long when she goes back home [to Engelthal]. May God help us all!

Dear treasure, I ask you not to forget about my Italian coat, one like the one Wilhelm Imhoff brought his wife from Venice, which is worn as a fur. Do not think ill of me because I always try to wheedle something out of you in every letter. I especially ask that you bring some red and saffron-colored satin, if you can find an inexpensive measure or two. Brother-in-law Jörg says a package is coming to me in a trunk; I hope the material for the vest is what is on the way; I very much need it.

Later today I must be a dinner guest of old Frau Kleewein, who is entertaining the girl, her new daughter-in-law, who is going to stay with her for a while. In a week, God willing, we will celebrate brother Paul's betrothal. Would to God that you could also be here.

May Almighty God bring us together again in joy after this tedious separation that we all want to forget with his help!

Kind, dear treasure, I have nothing more to write at this time, only to send many friendly and warm greetings to your loyal heart. May the Lord God keep you in his grace. Many, many others, all of whom I cannot list, send greetings to you—Frau Gröser, Frau Scheurl, Herr [Hieronymus] Paumgartner—yesterday I gave him a note at an engagement party, he has been to see us and greets you—Frau Lochner, Frau Roemer, Wilhelm Imhoff, Plauen, [both] he and she—the list is just too long. So many danced with me this week at the Pfinzings' wedding [December 6]. They wished you the best and asked me when I last had a letter from you. I dissembled and said, "Last week," when it has already been three weeks! This for now!

*Magdalena Balthasar Paumgartner,*
*your loving housewife*

Magdalena never stopped her personal requests for
foodstuffs and for clothing. With greater or lesser regu-
larity, she begs sugar, cheeses, quinces, Zellernuts (from
Zell, near Würzburg), pears, sweet fennel, olive oil,
"green nuts," and "a ham or three." She was also very
fond of inexpensive fine white ruffled linen collars, very
popular among the urban ladies; she loved aprons and
pieces of scarlet, satin, velvet, and damask.

Magdalena also sought, mostly in vain, a number of
luxuries. Among them were Netherlands dishware, ivory-
handled knives, an alabaster pitcher (for which Balthasar
searched both Florence and Venice), and two ounces of
unspun (unspooled) Venetian gold thread. She made special requests for Arles silk for her own wardrobe. Once
she planned to make a silk vest to replace her "completely bad" damask one. Another time she ordered
enough silk for several new garments because "my
clothes are so bad around the arms that I dare not wear
them during the day, and I always have guests coming."
When the silk arrived, she was rhapsodic: "it is beautiful, thick, lustrous."

In the winter of 1591, Magdalena set Balthasar look-
ing for a special Italian fur coat, "like the one Wilhelm
Imhoff brought his wife from Venice." With the same
stroke of her quill, she begs Balthasar not to think ill of
her "because I always try to wheedle something out of
you in every letter," immediately adding a request for
red and saffron-colored satin. Balthasar ordered the coat
specially from Michael Imhoff in Venice. From Magdalena's description Balthasar believed the coat to be a
new model, certainly one he had never seen before. As
it turned out, the coat was not a new Venetian model,
since no record of it could be found among the Imhoff
orders sent from Venice to Nuremberg. Suspecting that
it came from Augsburg, Balthasar told Magdalena to try
to get more precise information.

Magdalena's vanity found charming expression in the

summer of 1584, when she was pregnant with little Balthasar. At the time, she asked Balthasar to send her four measures of damask so that she could make a buttonless dress, apparently a kind of loose shift, for herself. Although she claims she has never before worn such a dress gladly, she is now so large that she must. "When I go out, I can never button my vest, and I have let it out as far as I can. Were I any larger, I must benumb myself to button my clothes, and that I would not like to do! I want to conceal myself for a while with a dress."

When Balthasar succumbed to vanity, it was on a grander scale. During the summer of 1594 he went on a personal buying spree. Among his purchases was an expensive piece of blue-and-gold damask for a canopy bedcover. Through a colleague, Stephan Wacker, he also acquired a slightly used blue pavilion with all the trappings, containing an estimated one hundred yards of damask—a rare bargain, he believed, at thirty-three Italian crowns. Exactly what he intended to do with it is unclear; most likely it became a stall at the fair. He clearly believed he could sell it for a good profit. His most self-indulgent purchase was a new coat. With an eye toward winter, he decided to special-order from a Nuremberg furrier a "wolf coat" with black unfinished camel's-hair lining. The coat required six to seven wolf pelts ("depending on the size of the wolves") which Balthasar ordered from Poland, whence the best quality skins came. In these days Nuremberg applied its sumptuary laws—which were designed to maintain social hierarchy and order—as strictly to dress as to other materialist displays. In sixteenth-century burgher society, presumption in dress was believed to breed an internal spirit of rebellion. Just how seriously the control of dress was taken is indicated by the requirement, established in the late fifteenth century, that all men in the city, for propriety's sake, wear coats and mantles that extend at least two finger lengths over the fly. Law also regulated the amount and the cut of fur in a coat. Although wolf pelts were not among the restricted furs, Balthasar pointedly assured Magdalena, who observed dress codes almost as earnestly as she did medical directives, that "a great, pressing necessity, not pride," had forced him to make so striking an addition to his wardrobe.

## ❧ EQUALITY

MAGDALENA TO BALTHASAR
*21 January 1585, in Nuremberg*

Honest, kind, dearest Paumgartner:

I wish you a happy, joyous new year and everything in it that is useful and good to you in soul and in body from Almighty God, and as much for us all. Amen.

Kind, dear Paumgartner, if it is true, as Veit [Pfaud] tells me, that you will be arriving safe and sound in Leipzig, I count it a triumph in the management of your affairs. For it is today, as I write, just five weeks since you left. May Almighty God help bring us back together in love and joy! I thank the Lord God that your son and the members of the household are still in good health. May God continue to grant it!

Dear Paumgartner, I have received your letter from Braunschweig with heartfelt joy; I hope that with God's help you are now completely done there. I asked Veit [as to your whereabouts] and he proposed that I could write to you in Leipzig, if I wanted. Because of the new joy [in your family] I could not let pass the opportunity to write and wish you luck with a new brother-in-law. Just yesterday I dined with old Aunt Scheurl, her two sons, and their wives. Conrad Bair's son [Stephan] dined for the first time with your sister [Helena]. While you have been away, she has changed her status. I fear you will also miss their engagement party on the Friday before Candlemas [February 2].

You, dear Paumgartner, however, have a little reprimand awaiting you from old Scheurl, who is indignant that you did not properly inform her of these proceedings. Before you left, the marriage plans had almost been completed by Hieronymus Paumgartner and your father. Your father thought that since he had written to you about them, you had announced the marriage to Aunt Scheurl and Helena. The marriage would still be completely undisclosed to them had not Stephan Bair, innocently and in good spirits, asked Helena, your sister, if what had been arranged between them also pleased her as it did him. She was shocked; she had known nothing. He had also just sent her a little chain as a New Year's gift. When Helena got home she told Aunt Scheurl, to whom it was even more unknown. She quickly got up and set forth with Helena to your father, and there received her first proper account of the matter. He was puzzled why, after his letter to you, you had not announced the marriage to them. The matter has now been quickly resolved. Her [Aunt Schuerl's] two sons have just been to Schlackenwalde. They arrived here yesterday, just at the right time to keep the new bridegroom company. I must always write you something!

Dear Paumgartner, today they buried Sigmund Oertel, who has died.

I do not know anything else to write you at this time, dearest treasure. May God help bring us together soon, so that we may talk face to face for as long as we want. Presently I am busy making the bridegroom's crown for Helena['s wedding]. Aunt Scheurl is hosting the engagement party and also paying for it, but she will not pay for the wedding. One will not, however, want for anything; she is also giving her [Helena] 1,000 gulden.

No more at this time except to commend you to the Lord God. A hundred thousand friendly and sincere greetings from me! May the loving God keep you. And make the best, my dearest treasure, of my bad writing; I have written very hurriedly.

*Magdalena Balthasar Paumgartner*

When Magdalena and Balthasar comment on the marriages of others, as they frequently do, they make their
own marital values very clear. They disparage behavior
that contradicts their own experience of marriage as a
close partnership. Neither was accustomed to being taken
advantage of by the other, and they knew they could
depend on each other when it counted. They look critically on marriages exhibiting inequality or immaturity.

Heading their list of questionable marriages were those
with great disparity in age, a disparity of twenty years
or more, between the older man and his young wife.
When they married, Balthasar was thirty-two, five years
older than Magdalena, to them a very proper spacing.
Like Magdalena, Balthasar sympathized with the widow
Flexner, who had suffered under a stern older first husband. For her he wished "a handsome youth," "a pleasant fellow," "no more old men." Magdalena shared with
Balthasar an outspoken criticism of age disparity by another victim whose complaint she learned of from Frau
Gabriel Scheurl. The woman in question, a Hamburger,
had very recently married an Italian physician resident
in Nuremberg. While attending Siegfried Pfinzing's wedding, she sat beside Frau Scheurl at the table of the
bride. Despite the fact that she was a newcomer (she
had been in Nuremberg for only two weeks), the woman
filled Frau Scheurl's ear with her complaints about the
way she had been treated. "One gives me at forty-two
years of age to a man who is seventy, for whom I now
must care"—an arrangement that did not "half please"
her, nor Magdalena.

Balthasar and Magdalena also disapproved of too
youthful marriages. In 1534 Nuremberg had established
the legal ages of marriage without parental consent at
twenty-five for men and twenty-two for women. With
parental consent marriages could theoretically occur as
early as the canonical ages of fourteen (men) and twelve
(women), but marriages at such early ages were extremely rare. When Balthasar learned in 1583 of the

planned marriage of Hans Welser, a wealthy widower with many children, to a young neighbor, Maria Muffel, he was taken aback because of her youth. "I am amazed," he confides, "that she should so soon become a mother with many children." The comment was indeed a pregnant one. Assuming Maria was still alive in March 1597, it is she who, Magdalena reports then, has given birth to Hans Welser's twenty-sixth child. Magdalena winced when she learned that the widow Stockhamer, who was alone with nine children and obviously in need of assistance, had given her youngest and ostensibly more desirable daughter ahead of her eldest in marriage to Caspar Burkhart. "I believe people are not prepared to see a girl so young get married," she writes Balthasar, clearly expressing her own view of the marriage.

Magdalena was equally sensitive to speedy remarriage of widows and widowers, a mild social problem in the city. In 1561, widows headed 11 to 12 percent of Nuremberg households. Those with marriage portions and established businesses made attractive mates for new burghers eager to establish citizenship and move ahead in a trade or business. In the sixteenth century a middle-aged or older person long accustomed to the companionship of marriage might, if alone for an extended period, freeze, starve, or go mad. Both widows and widowers appreciated the purely utilitarian side of marriage and understandably remarried quickly. That such quick remarriages nonetheless disturbed the Nuremberg citizenry is made clear by a Council decree in December 1560 instructing jurists to find ways to enforce "a certain waiting period" on widows and prevent "too easy remarriages." Magdalena uses precisely the same language as the Council when in 1584 she criticizes a Herr Bosch as a "frivolous man" for marrying Felicitas Pömer just ten weeks after the death of his wife. "One should not forget so soon!" she exclaims to Balthasar, seeing the remarriage as a betrayal of love and loyalty.

Magdalena bristled at marriages arranged without full and prior consultation with the prospective bride (such had not happened to her), a practice not unheard of in Nuremberg. Normally a prospective bride joined her family in weighing the pros and cons of a proposed match, thereby assuring her consent to the marriage well in advance of its occurrence. According to William Smith, however, it "oftentimes" happened in Nuremberg that a prospective bride first learned of her marriage after the family of the prospective bridegroom had negotiated the union with her family—a practice Smith disapproved. Magdalena witnessed such a scenario when her sister-in-law Helena married Stephan Bair. The marriage had been initiated by the heads of the two families without consulting Helena, who was still left in the dark after the initial discussions ended favorably, because of a confusion between Balthasar and his father as to who would tell her. Helena first learned of the planned marriage accidentally when, at an arranged dinner, the prospective bridegroom innocently and eagerly asked her if she was as enthusiastic about the match as he. Helena had known nothing about it and she was "shocked." So she and her Aunt Scheurl, who was even more upset, flew off to find her father, from whom the pair got their "first proper account" of the marriage plans. The Bairs were family friends and customers, so Helena had known Stephan. He had just recently given her a small necklace for New Year's in anticipation of the announcement of their marriage, about which he, unlike Helena, had been fully informed from the outset. The issue for Helena was not a gratuitous imposition of an unknown or undesired mate by her family, but an equal role with the bridegroom in the decision-making process. Helena and, vicariously, Magdalena resented the discriminatory procedure, not the match, which occurred harmoniously three months later (March 9, 1585). In Magdalena's own married life, consultation with Balthasar had been commonplace on every issue of mutual interest; such equality, she believed, should also characterize a marriage's inception.

Magdalena's heart also sank at the thought of marriage to an undisciplined man. Having attended the Schmidmaier-Tucher wedding, which (untypically) she found "boring," she reports that the long day was capped by the groom's failure, or rather inability, to join his wife on their wedding night, because he had "gotten too drunk earlier in the day." "God forgive me, but I do not envy her," Magdalena sighed as she recalled the "rare event" of a poor wife alone at the table on her wedding night.

Magdalena praised independence in women and sensitivity in men. She approved when Jörg Bair's wife defended her honor by tenaciously tracing to the source a rumor that her husband was not the father of her child. When her brother Paul's first child arrived four weeks prematurely in 1592, the one salient fact Magdalena reported to Balthasar was that the anxious father "maintained himself extremely well."

Magdalena and Balthasar could only heap scorn on marriages that lacked a basic equality in ability and responsibility—marriages where one party was in a position to burden the other unfairly, or where one party acted independently of the other in matters affecting both, or where the maturity to manage in good times and to cope in bad seemed lacking in one or the other partner.

# IV

# PARENTS

## ❧ LITTLE BALTHASAR

MAGDALENA TO BALTHASAR
*23 March 1588, in Nuremberg*

Honest, kind, dear Paumgartner:
I could not let pass the opportunity to write you a short letter. I hope to God that you will have arrived safely [in Frankfurt] by Thursday next and that your hands by then are full. May God grant that it goes well and is a success!

I am, praise and thank God, still lively and well. As for little Balthasar, he remains as you left him. I took him to the doctor, who told me he definitely has a deformity [in his neck], perhaps given him by the midwife when I had him, when one limb was firmly swaddled over another. Since then he has grown that way, and the doctor cannot help him now because it is fixed in him, except that he [said he] would give me a salve, which he has done. I am supposed to rub it on him early in the morning and at night and also place a pad on his neck that prevents him from bending backward. I have had to pay 2 gulden for a little crucible of salve. May God help make it work! Little Balthasar will let no one rub it on him except the cook.

Know further, dearest Paumgartner, that [your] father, [step-] mother, and Hans Albrecht have been here from Monday through Friday. When Hans returns to Vienna in the next few weeks, he plans to marry a widow, one from the nobility with two children, in a place 10 miles* beyond Linz, before Vienna. May God give him success! Scheurl could hardly raise 20 Frankish crowns for him here, so frugal are they at the fair. He [Hans] would himself gladly be there [in Frankfurt] with you. Here he had bracelets, one chain, and three rings made. [Your] father has given him some of his own [wealth]. May God grant him a good increase from it! I think he will also write to you himself.

Please, dearest treasure, buy us the Old Testament with the Psalms and the Prophets, for we often need it. And do not forget linen, should you need some. Also get us a couple of cheeses. And do not forget the little hat for little Balthasar. He talks about it all day.

I do not have anything else to write at this time, dearest treasure, except to send you warm and friendly greetings and commend you to Almighty God. May he help us be together again in good health!

*Magdalena Balthasar Paumgartner*

Magdalena and Balthasar had one child, a son. Magdalena describes herself as "halfway" through a pregnancy in a letter written in July 1584, so the boy must have been born in November or early December of that year. He first appears in her letters when she reports to Balthasar in January 1585, ". . . your son and the members of the household are still in good health." From then on, every letter brings news of little Balthasar, and, as the years pass, there are occasional "letters" of a few lines from the boy himself. "Enclosed is a letter from your son," Magdalena announces in a March 1588 let-

* "2 meil." *A German* Meil *equals five English miles.*

*Nuremberg children at play, from a scene entitled "Chil-
dren's Dance" by Jost Amman. Amman was a resident in
Nuremberg during the lifetime of Magdalena and Balthasar,
from 1574 until his death in 1591.*
Reprinted from Walter L. Strauss, *The German Single-Leaf
Woodcut, 1560–1600,* vol. 1, p. 68, by permission of the editor
and Abaris Books, Inc.

ter; "he too wanted to write to you." Magdalena regularly paraphrases or passes along verbatim little Balthasar's messages to his father, which invariably make a special request or boast of some achievement or, at least, report earnest striving after some worthy goal. Little Balthasar's father was for him a man of near-magical powers. Over a three-year period he begged from him, with mixed success, such items as celery, stockings of many colors, purses, boots and spurs, clothing, an Italian crown hat, and, most plaintively, a horse. Little Balthasar also knew his father to be a man who demanded of others almost as much as he was capable of giving: a man who could please, he also had to be pleased. So the boy pestered his mother to keep his father abreast of his growing skills in writing and music and to assure him of his constant diligence and good behavior.

The child's requests provide windows onto the family's emotional life. Magdalena is advocate and sentinel for her son, reminding the absent father of the boy's worthiness and encouraging paternal recognition and praise. She never makes a negative comment about him. She understands, as her husband often does not, the boy's sensitivity when one of his requests is either ignored or summarily denied by his father. "You must have a satin purse made for little Balthasar," she writes urgently; "he tells me every night that you are bringing him one." "Little Balthasar warmly greets you, and he has charged me to ask you to bring him a pair of red stockings and a purse." "Little Balthasar wants only boots and spurs when he is asked what you should bring him. Now you know what you may bring him." "You may well be asking, 'Is that all?,' " Magdalena writes with amusement at the end of a list of her own requests. "So now comes a message from little Balthasar. He wants two pair of stockings, one of which, he says, must be like those the students in Altdorf wear. (He means flesh- or saffron-colored.) Do what you like about this." On another occasion Magdalena comments that her letter is written in response to little Balthasar's "constant admonishing" that she ask Father to bring him some new clothes.

Both father and son "charge" and "admonish" Magdalena, while she makes "requests" of them. Her "requests," however, are foxy, her deference is only mannered. Despite occasional disappointments, she is, on the whole, every bit as effective as her menfolk in getting her way, and her life, by her own strong conviction and by Balthasar's ready concurrence, is measurably happier and more self-fulfilling than his.

Magdalena devoted herself to little Balthasar's education and training. In early 1590, when the boy was nearing six years of age and ready to begin formal schooling, she writes that Balthasar should, when he returns from Frankfurt, see the schoolmaster about enrolling him in Latin school "so that he can learn to write well . . . he resists study; [playing in] the stable is doing him harm."

In 1591, little Balthasar started private music lessons which he attended each day after school. His mother describes them as a four-month experiment to discover the extent of the boy's talent. So far, she reports, the results have been excellent. Little Balthasar goes dutifully every evening and likes it. His teacher has told her that he has never had a pupil grasp the fundamentals so quickly. "Little Balthasar has just come in [from his music lesson] and said to me, 'Mother, write Father that I can already strike a tune on my instrument; and tell him I greet him warmly.' " With Magdalena's Christmas 1591 letter came two samples of little Balthasar's writing. "They are as well as he can do now," she writes more sympathetically than proudly; "it takes him a while to produce such samples." She describes his day as very full: a quarter day in Latin drills, followed by music lessons, then writing at night.

Balthasar's responses to his son's requests for gifts

and favors can only be described as manipulative. Not that he seems ever to have been intentionally uncaring or unloving; on occasion he could even surprise little Balthasar with a special gift. He made arrangements, for example, for the Frankfurt hatmaker Wirschhauser to make the five-year-old boy "a compact, proper little felt hat." Magdalena had sent, at Balthasar's request, a string measure of little Balthasar's head together with material for the lining of the hat, as its creation became a cooperative venture between them. As a rule, however, Balthasar treated gifts strictly as incentives for good conduct, using them to threaten the boy into behaving well. "Tell little Balthasar to be good for the time being, otherwise I will bring him nothing. If he is bad, I will give the beautiful satin purse, the two pairs of shoes, and the red striped stockings I have bought for him to another little boy who behaves better than he." "If little Balthasar is good, I will bring him the desired stockings like the ones the students in Altdorf wear; if he is not, I will bring him nothing." Twice in his letters he threatened the boy with the rod, and on one of these occasions he even raised the specter of expulsion: "Tell little Balthasar to be good, and that should I learn that he has been bad, I will bring him nothing but a good strong switch, and the next time I go away I will put him out to board with the schoolmaster." Balthasar also made it clear to his son that the quality of their relationship upon his return would depend on his behavior during his absence. "Tell little Balthasar to be good, otherwise we will settle accounts with each other when I return," he declares with the detachment of a merchant billing a client. Or even more sternly: "I would like you to tell little Balthasar to be very good and study diligently, otherwise we will not be friends and I will bring him nothing."

Magdalena understandably worried that Balthasar played too much upon the boy's emotions and did not realize the harsh impact his words and actions could have on little Balthasar's feelings. For a New Year's present in 1592, little Balthasar had set his heart on an Italian crown hat. Magdalena alerted Balthasar, who was then in Lucca, to the boy's desires in mid-November, promising a letter from little Balthasar on the subject. She, in fact, included a touching petition from the boy in this letter. "Dear Father," little Balthasar writes, "I beg you to send me an Italian crown to wear on New Year's; I will be good all the time and pray diligently for you." It is signed "Balthasla Paumgartner d.l.s. [Little Balthasar Paumgartner, your loving son]." His father had decided to delay this particular gift as an incentive to good behavior. His New Year's Day 1592 letter includes the following message: "Tell little Balthasar that when I return home and learn that he has been good and studied diligently, I will give him his New Year's gift personally."

The result of the father's withholding of the crown was a devastated child and an outraged mother.

Only little Balthasar among us has had his hopes dashed on New Year's Day. We had assured him that you would send him an Italian crown as a New Year's gift. When it did not arrive, he became completely despondent. I myself believe you should not have forgotten his New Year's gift. You could have brought him great joy. You *still* can do so with your next letter. I beg you, dear Paumgartner, that in the future you not ignore what I tell you in my letters.

Such conflict between Magdalena and Balthasar is unusual, and this episode stands out in the correspondence. They generally cooperated in child-rearing decisions, although Magdalena clearly took the initiative in the early years. When they disagreed, they tended to compromise, but on terms that favored the father. In December 1591 they were at odds over a jacket for little Balthasar. His father had contemplated an expensive saffron-colored damask jacket, which Magdalena, sensitive to Nuremberg's sumptuary laws, believed too expensive and feared might occasion criticism for extravagance and ostentation. She preferred a black jacket instead, especially since little Balthasar's two previous jackets had been colored. "Of course," she dutifully acknowledges, "in this matter it is yours to do as you please." In the end, Balthasar chose a white jacket for his son, with only a modest accommodation to Magdalena's concern. "I have had a white, I say white, jacket made for little Balthasar from a piece of material I got at a good price; the fabric is a satin, but a plain satin." A coordinated pair of ballooned saffron-colored damask Italian pants, however, completed the boy's new outfit, all of which Balthasar promised to bring to him "if little Balthasar is good and studies diligently."

High infant and child mortality were rampant in the sixteenth century; possibly one-third of all children died before the age of twelve. Little Balthasar was not spared his share of childhood ailments and diseases. During the infant years, he was often "fussy" because of "bulging eyes," ostensibly the result of infection (conjunctivitis) or blocked tear ducts, and chronic colds and coughing. In March 1588, when he was about four years old, a doctor diagnosed him as having an "impression," that is, a deformity or misshaping in his neck, which had resulted in a rigidity that prevented normal movement. Magdalena and the doctor blamed the malady on improper swaddling by a midwife during the first weeks of life. The doctor prescribed a salve which was to be rubbed into the affected area in the morning and at night. According to Magdalena, little Balthasar, demonstrating a four-year-old's well-known capacity for temperamental rigidity, refused to allow anyone but the cook to apply the medicine. Massaging with the salve proved to be effective; after two weeks of treatment Magdalena could report that he was "bending better."

However, full mobility, according to the doctor, would take a year of such treatment.

On April 1, 1589, Magdalena wrote Balthasar that "the little rascal" had been sick for ten days with a cough so hard and so deep that he regularly expelled blood through his mouth and nose. She describes the ailment as one presently afflicting many children and old people in Nuremberg. A year later little Balthasar fell victim to worms, passing, by Magdalena's count, over three hundred. "White Bohemian beer is his only comfort," she informs his father as she prays that a more effective purgative will be found to "drive the poison from his heart and stomach." "We must, as I have said before, always have a crisis or two during your absence." Later their doctor, who visited little Balthasar every other day (Magdalena had urged daily visits), concocted a special powder that succeeded in killing all the worms and eventually also broke the high fever.

To be a parent in early modern Europe meant constantly to watch and to worry. Magdalena remained especially vigilant to signs of fatigue in the boy, usually a good indicator of the onset of an illness. When such signs appeared, she kept little Balthasar at home and "out of the air." "He is very content to stay home from school," she assures his father in December 1591 when she discovers the boy to be so "completely wiped out" that it reminds her of the time he came down with measles.

In February 1592, little Balthasar fell seriously ill with worms and dropsy, ailments he had survived two years before. Magdalena writes to Balthasar, then in Augsburg, that she "longs for him [her husband] under my cross which God has again made us bear by afflicting little Balthasar." The boy's stomach was so swollen that he screamed day and night and was unable to urinate. Purgatives had been administered three times, but to no avail, since little Balthasar could not keep them down. Finally, Dr. Weler, one of at least two attending physicians, concocted a tasteless powder that little Balthasar successfully swallowed. Soon he passed "around five hundred" worms in four stools. The stomach infection persisted, however, despite the use of every known remedy, including having the boy drink "his old water," ostensibly some of his own urine. "May Almighty God still grant his grace," Magdalena pleads, reporting the "puzzlement" on the part of the doctors that they could not reduce the swelling and make him urinate. They finally placed their hope in enemas, herbal purgatives, and stomach plasters, none of which allayed the boy's pain. "May eternal God add his grace to the medicine, so that little Balthasar will have recovered by the time you return," she writes Balthasar. But it was not to be.

I wish I could send you happier news. I am writing now in the night as I stand watch in his room. Your father has also not been well . . . [Before little Balthasar fell ill] I had firmly decided to hitch up [your] father's three horses and ride with Christoph and your brother Paul to meet you in Augsburg so that I could see the city. . . . But our Lord God has again seized upon us so that Augsburg is now forgotten. May God help us soon to know joy again.

By March, the child had deteriorated to the point where Magdalena urged Balthasar to come home immediately, which he began making plans to do. "He sleeps day and night now," she writes, "but there is little hope that he will regain his health, only that he may revive. Pray that the merciful God may now show his mercy and help him according to his divine will."

His father had not been out of little Balthasar's thoughts during the illness. For a year preceding its onset, the boy had pleaded with his father to bring him a horse, at first a stuffed or toy horse, but eventually a real one. "Dear Father," he wrote in March 1591,

*A letter from Little Balthasar to his father, requesting a toy horse covered in calfskin.*
Reproduced by permission of the Germanisches Nationalmuseum, Hist. Archiv Rst. Nürnberg XVIII/4 Paumgärtner.

I am happy to hear that you have arrived [in Frankfurt] safe and sound. Please bring me a little pony. Ask Meringer [ostensibly a dealer] where you can buy one covered with cowhide. Also two pairs of stockings, one skin-colored and one black. I try to be good all the time and I study diligently. Make the best of my writing; I hope to do better soon.

Magdalena freely assisted the boy's campaign for a horse, and she alerted Balthasar to his son's rising expectations. "Please ask Meringer about horses," she writes in September 1591. "He knows where one can find horses covered with goatskin. The boy talks incessantly about a horse, but he [now] has in mind a small living one. You may wish to buy him one." In her Christmas 1591 letter, she reported that little Balthasar had drawn in his notebook "a lively horse amid a scene of great commotion," and she warned Balthasar that the boy would soon be pleading his case directly for a real horse. The illness that intervened in February 1592 did not diminish little Balthasar's ambition to have a horse. Magdalena reports that despite his being bedridden and almost totally incapacitated, "when I told him that I was writing to you, he said to me, 'Tell Father to bring me a real horse.' "

These were the last words Balthasar would receive from his son. Three days later, Magdalena sent news of his death:

Your letter arrived today, Wednesday, only a short time ago. In the great affliction so recently brought upon me by God, I had waited longingly for it on Monday. After I had written to you last Thursday, he [little Balthasar] had a very bad night, so bad that I did not leave his bed then or on the following night because his breathing had become so difficult and continued that way until Saturday noon. All the while he was constantly talking, although not in such a way that any could understand him. Finally he wanted to get out of bed. Seeing that he was too weak to do so, we started to lift him up, whereupon he began to convulse. Within a quarter hour he was dead. . . . May God now keep him safe until we come to him!

Magdalena had the body immediately autopsied, and thereafter she reported to Balthasar the surgeon's discovery of a liver and kidneys so grotesquely enlarged that all the doctors marveled that the boy had lived so long.

What now was left for the parents? Having watched so great a part of her life end so tragically, Magdalena bares her soul to Balthasar.

I must now accept these facts: that we had him for so short a time, that he has not really been ours [but rather God's], and that we have unfortunately known in him a short-lived joy. I must accept God's will and let him go in peace to God, for there is nothing left in this for me now except suffering, heartache, and tears. I must learn to block it from my mind as best I can and you must do the same, my heart's treasure. You must strike it from your mind and be patient. Perhaps God will again be merciful to us and help us to forget this now that he has afflicted us so much. I know that if you were here all my suffering would be so much easier! For me every day now becomes as three. I trust you will make your way home in advance of the [merchants'] convoy, if you possibly can. I worry, however, that when you receive this tragic news from cousin Paul Scheurl's letter and from mine you will not want to hurry home ahead of the convoy. I will, however, hope better of you. May God help us to be together again in joy and without any more misfortune. I know from your letter that the Lord God has helped you make your way safely there; may he now grant you a good fair. I have faithfully buried our son as one who now lives in another body that knows no human suffering. Too early the clergy and the choir carried him away, too soon the bells were tolled for him.

In conclusion, Magdalena asked Balthasar to "send new wine, because we now have entirely too strong wine to drink every day." The request was an ordinary one; as their wine aged and soured, she routinely asked for new. Did she comprehend the deeper meaning of the request on this occasion, or was it lost on her in her grief?

# ❖IN LOCO PARENTIS:
# MADELA BEHAIM
# AND JÖRG IMHOFF

### MAGDALENA TO BALTHASAR
*6 June 1594, in Nuremberg*

Honest, kind, dearest Paumgartner:
Since I last wrote you two weeks ago, your other letter has been received and I am happy to learn from it that you have begun to purge yourself. Always the sooner, the better! If you have started in hot weather, may the Lord God continue to give you his divine blessing! If you are now going daily into the bath, may God grant that it do you good! Praise God, the bleeding of my arm has been entirely good for me. The swelling in my shoulder about which I have so long complained is now gone, praise and thank God!
A week ago I was preparing to write to you when brother Friedrich unexpectedly arrived and wanted me to go home with him, as his little one was again fully recovered from measles.* So I went immediately with him and have been there for five days. Praise God, the time passed quickly for me among the children, and I

---

* Flecken *may connote smallpox rather than measles. The basic connotation is spots, discolorations, or breaks in the skin, with or without fever. Measles is the primary connotation. Three weeks earlier, Magdalena had hoped to bring Madela home with her. However, all of Friedrich's children were at the time down with measles.*

then took little Madela, who is a year and four months old, back home with me. We all had such fun with her there. She is so amusing. [Traveling home] she runs about the coach like a little monkey. I hope soon, within a month or two, she will be able to go about unassisted. Dearest treasure, this week the Duchess of Pommersfelden sent me 30 gulden, sparing me from having to write her for it.

On Sunday, young Andreas Imhoff returned from Augsburg. I do not know when [Paul] Praun will reappear [from Italy] and build our coach.

Early today the Netherlanders* again sold cloth from their warehouse. [Paul] Scheurl and your brother Jörg were there; they had earlier bought a piece for dyeing. Scheurl says an arm's measure sold for around 16 pazen [batzen].† I had to pay the tailor 16 pazen a measure [when I recently] bought 5 measures for a coat. Had I known earlier that they [Paul and Jörg] would be buying some, I would have waited; but it has now already been done.

[Your] father is as he was. I do not know what their plans are. [Your] father himself wants to come here on St. Lawrence's Day. But Herr Paumgartner cannot leave the house; he cannot do anything. I still wonder how much longer he can last.

I do not know much other news for you, kind, dear Paumgartner, except that Bernhard Kötzler is the bridegroom of Fräulein Brechtel. Herr [Hieronymus] Kress is still determined to go to Hungary [and fight the Turks] in two weeks. He spent a week and three days at the Imperial Diet and his resolve was completely confirmed. May God help him and his little children.

Kind, dearest Paumgartner, I have no more to write at this time. Take many, many sincere and warm greetings from me into your heart of hearts, and may the Lord God keep you in grace.

*Magdalena Balthasar Paumgartner,*
*your loving Magdel*

* Dutch clothmakers resident in Nuremberg.
† A batzen was equal to 14 pfennigs.

BALTHASAR TO MAGDALENA

*20 July 1594, in Lucca*

Honest and kind, dear Magdel:

I wrote you most recently a week ago and sent along with my letter a quarter ounce of safflower-colored silk [thread]. Since then your letter of June 20 has arrived and the news that you and all of ours are healthy and well has been most happily received. For this I am thankful to dear God; may he continue to preserve us according to his gracious will.

I have since sent the other three-quarters ounce of safflower-colored silk to you in our crate number 84. I have written to my brother Jörg to ask him to deliver it to you as soon as it arrives, which might be two weeks after [your receipt of] this letter.

For his wife's sake I am especially happy to learn that Wilhelm Kress can still be moved by entreaty and remains at home.*

Paul Scheurl wrote me already before your letter that our flax has at last begun to arrive. We have, however, planned poorly; the next [order] from Lübeck should be shipped [to Nuremberg] by water; for it would have sold quickly and at a good profit [had it arrived sooner].

Herr Andreas Imhoff has this week written me a long letter about his son Jörg, in which he is very hard on him. He also indicated that I should read the letter to Jörg, which I have done with Jörg crying along. I am now answering [Andreas], and, besides [reporting] necessary [business] matters, I am assuring him that if he needs Jörg in their firm and will assign him a position in their warehouse beside a trusted man or servant whom Jörg fears and respects and who is also a strict schoolmaster, as Wilhelm and Andreas have had in Isaac Greck, then he can be employed right away and assigned writing and [other] tasks, which I am very hopeful he will fulfill to Andreas' every expectation.

* *That is, instead of going off to the Turkish war zone with his brother Hieronymus. Wilhelm was married to Magdalena's sister Sabina.*

For there is so far no reason to complain especially harshly about him. His father writes and begs that he not be allowed to do anything improper, or to wear expensive or silk clothing, all of which happened before; however, Jörg does not now want to do these things. I will gladly do my best with him and try in the short time I have remaining here to mold him so that he will be useful in any office.

I have nothing else to write you at this time, kind and dear Magdel. Many warm and sincere greetings; may the lord God keep you in grace.

> *Your loyal, loving husband,*
> *Balthasar Paumgartner, the Younger*

Magdalena could not put little Balthasar out of her mind. The most casual associations brought his memory rushing to the surface. Six months after his death she greets Balthasar, again at the Frankfurt fair, with the hope that they may soon "come together again in joy," but hastens to add: "—although God has now made a painful tear through our joy. In the past [when little Balthasar was alive] we have always been able to reunite with greater happiness than will unfortunately happen now." In the same letter, Magdalena reports the birth of a fifth son to the Hieronymus Kresses and exposes a gaping maternal wound: "[With five boys] they could well give one to us, if it were permitted." In May 1594, the need for a new coat reminds Magdalena of her pregnancy ten years earlier. She recalls that the coat she had then was so tight under the arms and on the sides that she was unable to wear it on a visit to the Jakob Imhoffs. When in the same year Balthasar informed her from Lucca that his Italian doctor had insisted that he regularly "purge" himself (that is, be bled), Magdalena shot back: "I applaud your doctor, for did we not unhappily see so clearly in our blessed child

the consequences of a stopped-up liver?" Her memory of
the child was still bright three years later when she sent
Balthasar a remedy for an ear infection. She recommended penetrating the ear three times a day with vapors from a sponge saturated with marjoram, lavender,
camomile, and wormwood mixed in equal portions of
wine and water—a recipe, she recalls, that "always
helped little Balthasar."

Part of the void in Magdalena's life came to be filled
by her niece and namesake, Madela, her brother Friedrich's child. Beginning in the spring of 1594, when
Madela was sixteen months old, she became a frequent
visitor in her aunt's home, a relationship encouraged by
Friedrich, who understood the sadness in his sister's life
and hoped to alleviate it. Friedrich's wife had just delivered a fifth child, so Madela's visits with her aunt
also helped Magdalena's sister-in-law. Magdalena throve
on the child's presence, much to Balthasar's delight.
"Boredom would overcome me were it not for Madela,"
she writes in the summer of 1594.

God preserve us, she is such a delightful thing, and like
a little monkey. She does not yet go about completely
on her own, but must hang on to someone or something
[when she walks], but she is very nimble. And she is
so very friendly. When Jörg Paumgartner comes, she
claps her hands and runs to him. I believe she thinks
he is her father.

Magdalena indulged the girl much as she had indulged
little Balthasar. She orders saffron-colored silk from
Italy for a bonnet; she instructs Balthasar to buy Madela
a dress. She watches the child pick up and study leaves,
and she describes going shopping and to church "with
my little chattering Madela." After a description of her
own weekly activities, Magdalena typically concludes a
letter: "Otherwise, I pass the time with little Madela,
who is so playful; we all enjoy her so."

Balthasar received greetings from Madela in Magdalena's letters along with news of her health and activities. As the years passed, he occasionally sent greetings back to her in his letters, although he never did so as faithfully or as fully as Magdalena wished. "Madela says that I should greet Uncle warmly," Magdalena writes in the spring of 1596, delivering through the child an old and very personal message: "She must be watching what I am doing, because there is nothing in your [last] letter for her."

A void had also been created in Balthasar's life by the death of his son, although he was not one to show it as openly as Magdalena. His paternal needs found another outlet and his parental talents another test when in 1594 Jörg Imhoff, the seventeen- or eighteen-year-old son of Andreas Imhoff, became his apprentice in Lucca. Jörg had been sent there by his father to continue his preparation for a place in the Imhoff firm. Jörg was spoiled and undisciplined, according to his sister Marina, who described him to Magdalena as "very petulant." It was in April 1594 that she begged Magdalena to ask Balthasar to take Jörg in hand, "because Jörg is a bit more fearful [of Balthasar] than he is of the staff there." Balthasar first got to know Jörg that spring while the young man was settling into the house in Lucca. Balthasar suspected Jörg of lying about his activities and whereabouts. He shared with Magdalena the discovery that Jörg, who was seldom around, had not been attending math lessons as he claimed; Balthasar learned from Jörg's music teacher that his math tutor had inquired about him because he had not seen him in a long time.

Balthasar was very pleased, however, to learn from a colleague, Stephan Wacker, that Jörg feared and respected him. This, Balthasar learned, was the reason why he was always so quiet in the house, and so eager to be out of it, when Balthasar was there. Balthasar believed that such fear and respect would enable him to restrain and mold the young man. His tactic in reining him in was very simple: heavy doses of the merchant's regimen. He kept Jörg busy writing and copying so that he had few idle moments to indulge his youthful whims. The Italian maid also brooked no nonsense from Jörg. She anticipated his mischief and countered it so effectively that Balthasar often found himself secretly laughing. When Jakob Welser the Younger left Lucca for the baths, Jörg had one fewer fellow scamp to run around with and more time to spend working.

Within a month Jörg's behavior improved, and Balthasar reported real progress in his acquisition of the merchant's skills. Since knowledge of foreign languages was a key part of the foreign apprenticeship, Balthasar began to dictate regularly to Jörg in Italian. Increased contact with Balthasar and the intensified professional training seem to have spurred the young man's maturation. "He fears and respects me and this has enabled me to restrain him," Balthasar writes. "He now addresses me politely and not rudely. But a certain number of years must pass for a mind to mature. I have begun to dictate my Italian letters to him, a task which he gives himself readily to and performs well; it will also help him in writing and speaking Italian. If all continues to go as it has begun, his father can be a very satisfied man."

Andreas Imhoff was prepared to make other arrangements for Jörg if the young apprentice failed to demonstrate aptitude for the merchant's trade, so he was eager to have Balthasar's evaluation. Jörg had to listen to Balthasar read a letter from his father highly critical of his past attitude and performance. Balthasar describes the letter as "very hard" on the young man, who listened in tears. Urged, unnecessarily, to subject Jörg to the most careful discipline, Balthasar assured Andreas that Jörg would have the ability to serve his father's firm well if he were placed under a "strict schoolmaster" whom he also respected. Balthasar obviously had in mind someone like himself. The letter pleased Andreas, who, thus reassured, gave Jörg permission to travel to Genoa with Balthasar, both a broadening of Jörg's training and a new personal adventure on which Jörg had wanted to embark.

Balthasar's success with Jörg pleased Magdalena, who praised his skills as a mentor. In a typically perceptive analysis of Andreas' stern paternal bearing, she expressed a sentiment that was probably true of early modern fathers generally, certainly of Balthasar during his years as an active parent. "Perhaps Andreas is so strict with Jörg," she points out, "because he does not want a failed child. Many fathers want more of their children than they often get."

# V

# SURVIVORS

Good health obsessed Magdalena and Balthasar. Magdalena, especially, swore by her doctors and trusted medical providence as much as divine. All around them friends and relatives fell victim to disease and accident, constantly reminding them of their own vulnerability. "I must report to you a death among our friends in every letter," Magdalena writes in the summer of 1584; "I wish it were not so." Her reports of the sick and dying in Nuremberg fall as steadily and as matter-of-factly as a gravedigger's shovel. Her descriptions are graphic and pathetic, the accounts of a helpless eyewitness. About Frau Gabriel Nützel, Balthasar's aunt, we learn "there is no longer any hope of her improvement, only of her salvation." Frau Behaim cries uncontrollably each night from the pain of incurable urinary disease. Frau Tobias Kastner wastes away with consumption, blood flowing from her mouth. Poor Gruner, the Roggenbachs' sister's child, drinks bottle after bottle of red wine to deaden the pain of a gangrenous foot from which he has no hope of recovering; his father stands at the window and sighs as each new bottle is opened. Frau Martin Haller's dysentery has ended in horrible, convulsive death. In September 1592, Balthasar's new gray horse joins Magdalena's list of casualties, a commentary on death's dexterity and the universality of the struggle for good health. Relatives, neighbors, and animals are read like the morning newspaper for signs of illness. Although her father-in-law would not die until August 1594, Magdalena begins reporting signs of his "imminent death" as early as September 1592. The constant morbid news left Balthasar convinced that his personal world was in a state of steady collapse.

The near-simultaneous deaths of his aunts Holzschuher and Nützel in 1584 moved him to complain that his uncle Paul Tucher was the only friend and counselor from his childhood who still remained alive (he would also outlive Balthasar). "We are constantly losing our best friends, one after the other." One such case that especially gripped Magdalena and Balthasar was that of Conrad Bair, a friend, a customer (Balthasar regularly supplied him with Miltenburg wine), and, after 1585, a relative (his son Stephan married Balthasar's sister Helena in that year). "Old Bair," as they affectionately called him, fell seriously ill in November 1591. Magdalena reports at that time that his bladder had failed and he had to be "pressed" to urinate. "As Georg Römer had what they call the 'cursed tubercles' in his rear [hemorrhoids], old Bair now has them in front, blocking his urinary tract"; he is described as being "greatly depressed." Within a week, he lost the use of his bowels as well, which, together with the arrival of a sudden bitter cold snap, made his death seem only a matter of days. From his bed, old Bair instructed Balthasar's brother Paul to take a blessing to their father and "tell him I will not see him again." "He has now said his goodbyes to everyone," Magdalena writes. On December 9, Magdalena predicted he would be dead within three or four days. "Every day some rotted flesh is cut away from his wound. He feels nothing, and he speaks only when he is thirsty or wants something." Two weeks later old Bair could not recognize Magdalena and had ceased altogether to eat and drink, "yet he seems amazingly unable to die." His lingering reminded Magdalena of the recently deceased Frau Huter, who also "lay half dead for a long time." Finally, on December 30, old Bair "took a beautiful end." The death made a particular impression on Balthasar, who mentions it on three separate occasions in subsequent months, expressing sympathy with Bair's suffering, regret over the loss of a "good, true friend," and the hope of his "happy resurrection."

## ❖STAYING ALIVE

MAGDALENA TO BALTHASAR
*7 July 1584, in Altdorf*

Honest, kind, most dear Paumgartner:

Your letter of June 25 has reached me in Altdorf and I understand from it that you have been drinking the waters for eight days and are doing better than others there.* As always, such news has brought me a special heartfelt joy. However, you must make up for the inadequate food and your lack of sleep and attend to your needs, sparing yourself nothing, when you return to Lucca. I have hoped that Almighty God will grant my heartfelt prayer and restore your health there by Christian means, since it has not been his will to do so here. May God preserve you at all times and bring you safely back to me in joy so that we may again cheer and comfort each other after our long separation.

I would surely like to know, if it is possible, whether you will depart Lucca before the fair and whether this is the last of my letters that I may expect will find you there.

* *Balthasar is taking the waters at the Luccan springs, a four- to five-hour ride from the city of Lucca itself.*

Kind, dearest Paumgartner, I had intended to leave Altdorf for home last Saturday, but your father would not let us go before his birthday, which he wants to celebrate on Wednesday morning. So we must remain here until Thursday, when, God willing, we will be home again.

Last Wednesday evening I dined with a great spoon [that is, royally] at the home of the Count in Altdorf. He had invited us to the wedding of his cook, but as we were taking care of Frau Nützel and could not attend, he asked us to come in the evening. They had many courses but little to eat, as the food was so God-awfully prepared in their Polish manner.

Friday I visited Frau Kastner in Engelthal. Herr Haller would not let us leave until noon, so we had to spend the night with him. I have also been to Hersbruck and from there back home again on Saturday to Altdorf, where happily I found your letter. So I must write to you again from Altdorf.

I am, praise God, doing well. Food and drink taste good to me, and I can drink wine again. I have not been drinking beer [in place of wine] in order to save money, as you perhaps think. I understand from your letter that I could not save much money by doing so anyway, even if I wanted to. I am, praise God, completely better now, and there lives in me what is yours and mine* given us by God. I have now, praise God, safely passed through half my time; may God let me also pass through the other half in good health.

Know, dear Paumgartner, that during the week I was away Frau Georg Volckamer departed in God. I must report to you a death among our friends in every letter I write; I wish it were not so.

Dear treasure, I can think of nothing more to write to you at this time, save that your father, [step]mother, brothers, and sisters all send sincere greetings. Receive, dearest treasure, many thousand greetings from me. May God keep you.

* Magdalena was at this time pregnant with little Balthasar.

I had completely forgotten to tell you that we are invited in two weeks to attend the wedding of Veit [Pfaud]'s brother in Neuenmarkt. When Pfaud arrives there, will you ask him to excuse us. I may not write any more; I have written too much. Jörg says Veit is ready [to depart] within the week, so I must make this short. May the Lord God protect you from suffering and harm. Amen.

*Magdalena Balthasar Paumgartner*

What could one do to preserve life and limb in an age so constantly besieged by disease and death? Magdalena and Balthasar had plenty of medical information and practical advice. There were the oral traditions derived from generations of experience, and the printed public counsel of the city's physicians. Kaspar Hochfeder's purging calendar, published in Nuremberg in 1496, gave the most auspicious times to be bled, one of the most popular preventive measures in Magdalena and Balthasar's circle. Manuals on bloodletting designed for physicians and bath surgeons, but of interest to all, circulated widely, providing detailed instruction on optimal bleeding points and procedures. Around 1550 an abridged vernacular edition of Andreas Vesalius' *Anatomia*, a book that attempted to describe every part of the body accurately, was published. By the late sixteenth century Nuremberg physicians had organized themselves into an official guildlike *collegium medicum*, which standardized treatments, regulated fees, and attempted to weed out quacks.

When plague or other disease threatened, the physicians routinely issued practical instructions on prevention. One popular pamphlet published in 1562 conveys the physician's self-image and the tactics he employed to gain public confidence. Entitled "A Brief Instruction on How One Should Behave in Time of Plague," it preaches both medical self-help and religious faith, em-

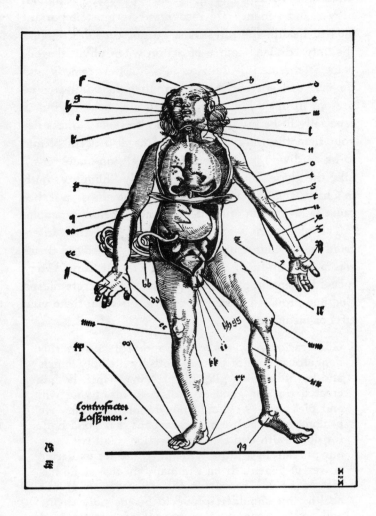

*A surgeon's chart of 1552 indicating the body's bleeding points. Magdalena speaks only of being bled from her arm, apparently at the bend in her forearm.*
From Johannes Charethanus, *Wundartznei zu allen Gebrechen des gantzen Leibs und zu jedem Glied . . . Rechte Kunst und bericht der Aderlass* (Frankfurt a.M., 1552). Reprinted by permission of The British Library.

phasizing specific actions and medicines one can take under the guidance of a skilled physician. Although prayer and penance are recognized as most important aids to health, the physicians do not consider religion the only "divine" course of action when physical well-being is threatened. Religion is a constant remedy and the cure of last resort, something that should always be present in one's life, even when one is healthy, but is especially to be invoked when all else fails. No less devout than the clergy, the physicians also deem plague to be "a divine punishment for our all-too-many sins." Like the clergy, they believe that only "humility, faith in Christ, and moral renewal" can in the end stop it, because God will not spare defiant and impenitent people.

The physicians were not, however, primarily interested in obvious truths and ultimate remedies; theirs was a profession of tangible and present cures. They focused attention on the immediate and concrete means God had provided to save and protect people: the divine gifts of medicine.

God graciously wants to save and protect us in this dangerous time [of plague] both by his holy angels and by his healing gifts of medicine, which he has created for our good according to his divine will and pleasure. We should not doubt that when we prolong our lives by medical means it is good both for our health and for our salvation. God will hear our prayers in a fatherly manner and let us derive powerful benefits from the many medicines he has blessed by his Word for the preservation of our health. But should it prove to be his holy divine will and pleasure to take us out of this troubled life, let us not doubt that sin, death, the Devil, and hell will surely be overcome and eternal life happily gained through faith in his dear son, our Lord Jesus Christ.

A similar physicians' instruction appeared at the onset of plague in 1572. It describes the medical arts in language ordinarily reserved for the sacraments of priests. The practice of medicine is presented as God's "ordained means" of health; a patient in the hands of a skilled physician is said to be in the very hands of God.

> Should one in time of disease be overcome with weakness, let him not lose heart and despair, but with sure trust in God turn immediately to the means God has ordained to help him, not only praying to God, but also seeking out the counsel and help of skilled physicians. . . . Herophilus spoke truly when he said that all medicines are useless if they are in the wrong hands, while the hands that know how to use them properly may be compared to the hands of God.

Nuremberg's physicians gave by and large sensible advice, much of which Magdalena and Balthasar methodically follow. Since disease is spread by direct physical contact, the most fundamental preventive act is careful avoidance of the afflicted, their dwellings, clothes, and bedcovers, as well as the baths and other public places where the sick and diseased assemble. Breathing the same air also put one in jeopardy, so thorough ventilation of closed spaces is deemed essential within infected areas. Stress is laid on conscientiously keeping one's home "clean and sanitary," advice difficult to follow during the bitter winter months, when spittle, urine, and other foul matter are collected on floors and walls. A continuous fire is recommended to prevent the collection of cold, moist air, which is a natural ally of disease because it weakens the body's resistance. Believing that good odors repel disease-laden bad odors, the physicians recommend frequent bathing with sweet-smelling rosewater and advise that apothecary "spiced apples" be worn in the streets. "Noble stones," like hyacinths or sapphires, also win endorsement as effective charms against disease.

Among the personal habits said to be conducive to

survival in time of plague, none is deemed more helpful than sobriety. Only a fool eats, drinks, and makes merry in time of plague. "The opinion of the commonfolk that one should be constantly eating and never sober in periods of pestilence is dead wrong," the physicians warn. Heavy foods, such as pork, sauerkraut, and many fruits, and strong drink are said to create unnatural moisture in the body, which putrifies the stomach and predisposes to disease. Light eating and drinking, even fasting, are the more prudent course. Also to be avoided when plague threatens are sexual activity and the emotions of anger and melancholy. These emotions, especially melancholy, are said to upset the humors, weaken the body, and invite illness. Here may be a source of Magdalena's hypersensitivity to Balthasar's talk about "anger between us" controlling their relationship at one point during their engagement. Such medical theories may also have been a factor in her frequent efforts to cheer him up when he was traveling.

In early modern medical practice, purgation complemented avoidance and abstinence. As the collection of foul matter in the body was believed to be the major cause of disease, regular flushing of the body became the most important prevention. Hence the physicians' recommendation of frequent use of enemas and suppositories and—Magdalena's favorite health measure—periodic bleeding, so long as the body is strong and healthy.

When Balthasar traveled, Magdalena worried constantly that an unexpected storm or illness might end his life. She reports to him her "terror" upon learning of the sudden death of Sebald Welser from dysentery in Ulm in September 1589, a tragedy made all the more pitiable to her because he left a wife who was four months pregnant. "I thought immediately of you, of your comment to me in our chamber, when you said that something would likely soon befall you while you were traveling. I am hoping that you have with God's help already safely arrived. . . . I want now only to learn of your well-being." Magdalena returned to the subject of Welser's death in her next week's letter, exclaiming: "May God spare me from such bad news as long as I live!"

Knowing Balthasar to be a worrier and a workaholic who skipped or skimped at meals, Magdalena feared that his bad habits would diminish his strength, lower his immunity, and leave him easy prey to foul weather or disease. Hence the steady reminders not to travel on an empty stomach. When she hears that plague is spreading along the Rhine, she pleads with him to go directly to an apothecary and get "something" to protect himself against "bad air" (a spiced apple or orange is meant). Most of all, she wants him to be bled regularly, in her estimation the supreme prophylaxis, the surest way to rid the body of the excessive and harmful fluids in which disease breeds.

Magdalena's enthusiasm for bleeding was universal in her time. In the sixteenth century it was not unusual for families and friends to take a kind of bleeding holiday, going together in groups to the bath surgeon and thereafter convalescing in leisure and play. The risks of bleeding are more obvious to us than they were to Magdalena's contemporaries, although critics did exist. The well-known physician Hippolytus Guarinonius was one of the most outspoken. He looked down on the professionally inferior bath surgeons as quacks who more often than not bled their clients into unconsciousness by opening as many as five veins at one time and caused many deaths by confusing arteries with veins. Magdalena had no qualms about the practice; indeed, she believed that the risks of not being bled far exceeded any posed by regular bleeding. She constantly nags the flagging Balthasar on the matter. When, in the spring of 1584, she learns that his health is failing, "bleeding at the first opportunity" becomes her plea. In November

1591, she reminds him that his time to bleed has come, pointing out that eleven weeks have passed since he left Nuremberg, apparently also that long since his last bleeding. Happily she reports that their Nuremberg surgeon has told her that "far more bleeding cups" exist in Lucca than in Nuremberg, "so you need not fall prey to bad humors there." Magdalena's admonition suggests that she and possibly also Balthasar bled themselves as often as four times a year, and almost always in Nuremberg. This would be double the recommendation of Guarinonius, who decries people who bleed themselves as frequently as twice a month. The Nuremberg physicians' instruction of 1572 recommended a regular cycle of spring and autumnal bleeding as optimal for good health.

Magdalena brims with personal testimonies to the curative power of regular bleeding. In November 1591 she reminds Balthasar for the second time within the space of a week to be bled, this time prodding him with an account of her own misfortune when she recently got off schedule. Exceeding her bleeding date by two weeks, she found herself suddenly unable to move her upper torso—hips, shoulders, and arms—freely. A heat-producing salve restored movement; however, the experience, she assures Balthasar, has taught her never again to procrastinate. After little Balthasar's death from a "stopped-up liver," she became near-evangelical on the subject. Two years later she claimed that regular bleeding had completely cured rheumatism in her shoulder.

In the end, Balthasar did his duty. When Magdalena learned he had been bled in Lucca per her instruction, she reinforced the deed by recounting the sad bleeding history of the terminally consumptive Frau Kastner. Before her marriage, Frau Kastner had bled herself regularly to control an inflammation in and around her eyes. After her marriage, she stopped going to the surgeon, as her eyes had gotten better. In truth, according to the woman's doctors, the inflammation had only moved from her eyes into her lungs, where it now placed her at death's door. Frau Kastner was presently being bled by her physician in an apparent eleventh-hour effort to stop her deterioration. Magdalena was frequently at her bedside and witnessed two bleedings in as many weeks, after which she claims Frau Kastner stopped vomiting blood and became somewhat stronger. Within a month of this report, however, Magdalena again described her condition as "hopeless"—and without any further mention of the wonders of bleeding.

# ❧BETWEEN GOD AND THE PHYSICIAN

BALTHASAR TO MAGDALENA
*5 June 1591, in Carlsbad near Schlackenwalde*

Honest and kind, dear Magdel:
    If you and ours are still well, cheerful, and healthy, I would most gladly hear it. I am eager to learn how the planned purging [bloodletting] agreed with you and little Balthasar. For my part, I am giving thanks to dear God. You may perhaps already have learned from cousin Christoph Scheurl in advance of my letter that I have, praise God, safely arrived here. Dr. Rubinger told me that, as he had a courier going there [to Nuremberg], he sent a letter to him [Scheurl]. I knew nothing of this courier; otherwise I would also have sent a letter to you. Because the way to Eger en route to Schlackenwalde had become so treacherous, I reconsidered and, to save time, chose another route to the bath. I arrived safely, praise and thank God, last Monday after vespers, having traveled a rather bad road with tired horses and [my] lazy, slow [servant] Cuntz.
    I rested on Tuesday and purged [with laxatives] on

*An engraving by G. Hupschmann of the hot springs at Carlsbad in the second half of the sixteenth century. Balthasar visited the springs in the summer of 1591. The springs with their rising hot vapors are visible in the center. Wooden canals carry the waters to bath houses on the right and the left that were segregated according to sex. A separate, unroofed bathhouse was maintained for the "scabby and leprous" (foreground, far left).*
From Alfred Martin, *Deutsches Badewesen in vergangenen Tagen* (Jena, 1906), p. 336.

Wednesday. Then on Thursday, the day before yesterday, I began to drink the waters in God's name. They have not yet, praise God, caused any bad effects. I sincerely hope that the journey, time, and expense will not prove to have been in vain. I purged quickly, but without any pain. I am able and permitted to drink a lot at one time; however, I hope that tomorrow I will still receive three liters and that that amount may remain the most for one day. As for when I will be able to leave here, I know and can tell you nothing at this time, for in this and other matters I must now live somewhat at the mercy of the doctor. I worry that one day may soon stretch into ten, but time will tell.

Herr Hans Köppel wrote me from Schlackenwalde last Wednesday and honored me with a rabbit. He offered me his good services, [saying] that I should write to him about my needs and that although at this time there is little to be had, he would do his best. I therefore directly asked him to send some young chickens, a batch of which arrived day before yesterday at 17 to 18½ pfennigs each. They were very small and included several old hens. Otherwise, this is a truly miserly bath, where money buys one nothing at all. There is neither wine nor beer with which to pass the time in the bath more moderately and pleasantly. In addition, we are completely bored with one another, as I have neither shirts nor any other article of clothing to wear and I have not yet left my room. As for my luggage and possessions, things are topsy-turvy for me, because I still have not received them. Day before yesterday Herr Köppel bid the coachman to be here today, and one sees what happens. Am I still in need of my trunks? Observe for yourself!

Our servant, the truly slow and lazy Cuntz, is not such to me. I wish I had never seen him. I now must find another to take his place. I want to ask the stablemaster what he thinks about the man who has been with young Andreas Imhoff and [who has] also [worked] with him in the stables. If we are able to take a ride together on Friday and I can get his opinion, I have already decided to let Cuntz go and take this one in his place. The stablemaster was not home today; he had just ridden into the field [when I called].

If the tailor has not yet finished or sent Father's coat, send to him for it, and have it sent on to Father in Altdorf.

In disbursing the grain, remember to calculate once altogether whatever is given to Father.

Tell little Balthasar to behave himself, and that should I learn that he has been bad I will bring him nothing but a good switch, and the next time I go away I will put him out to board with the schoolmaster.

If you can find a good, true, mature wine, you may certainly take a barrel home for us.

If Andreas Herling has still not paid his 17½ gulden Wöhrd rent, warn him about it. After the ruling of the court in Wöhrd, Hieronymus Herbst's debt is 28 gulden, 3 kreuzer, and several pfennigs, two gulden of which I have remitted. If this has not been made right, have my brother-in-law von Plauen warn him.

Dear, kind Magdel, I have nothing more to write, save to extend my sincere greetings to cousins Paul Scheurl and his wife, your brothers and sister Maria, brother-in-law [Wilhelm] Kress and his housewife, good friend Conrad Bair, and brother-in-law Stephan Bair and his wife. To you and little Balthasar, I send many friendly and sincere greetings. May the Lord God keep us all in his grace.

*Your loyal, loving husband,*
*Balthasar Paumgartner the Younger*


If Magdalena's medical faith was in bleeding, Balthasar's was in the waters of thermal springs. The period of their correspondence includes four visits to the baths—two (1584, 1594) to the mountain springs of Lucca, twenty miles from the city and a four- to five-hour journey; one (1591) to Carlsbad; and one (1596) to the cold springs of Langenschwalbach that lay along

Balthasar's route home from the Frankfurt fair. Balthasar's descriptions of his water cures provide a rare first-
hand account of sixteenth-century bath culture and
medical practice. They are particularly revealing of lay
attitudes toward medicine at a time when it asserted
itself as a profession and placed its mandate and power
to heal on a plane with religion. The lay responses to
the physicians, as exemplified by Balthasar and Magdalena, run a spectrum from exasperation to desperate
trust.

Balthasar's first recorded visit to the Luccan springs
occurred in the summer of 1584 after two trips to Genoa
in oppressive summer heat had left him completely exhausted. He seems also to have lost a lot of weight,
because he writes upon his arrival in Lucca that he needs
to "fatten" himself. Luccan friends and associates recommended that he recuperate by drinking the water
from the springs. Initially, Balthasar planned simply to
drink imported spring water, but he became convinced
that the water at the source would be much more potent.
So with the greatest reluctance he resolved to leave his
preferred work for a week and pursue his good health
in what he had been assured was the "paradise" of the
springs. He writes Magdalena on the eve of his departure with characteristic lack of enthusiasm for a new
venture and also with a naiveté about the baths that
will not be repeated.

Although I find the company of the burghers here completely satisfying, I will spend a week there [at the
mountain springs] and have the good life in paradise,
bringing to a close my life here below. Disregarding the
fact that I can ill afford to be away from my business,
where there is plenty to do and where my hands are
full, I must tackle a mountain in a valley and make a
virtue out of necessity. May the Almighty lend me his
grace so that it may turn out well for me! Most of the
people here who visit the bath do so only for the sake

of pleasure, taking the waters now so that thereafter they can eat and drink all the more exuberantly. That is not the case with me. Were it not necessary [for my health] to go, I would stay here and attend to the pressing matters [of my business]. I must have the good life totally against my will.

The cure at this time consisted only of resting and drinking the waters, two and one-third liters per day, early in the morning; Balthasar claims to have passed seven-eighths of it by noon, when he went out for the day. After three days of such purging, the most prominent effect he noticed was a "tumult" in his body. He felt none of the pain or the weakness that often accompanied the purging. His chief complaints throughout the stay are insufficient food and sleep. In the evening he is not permitted to eat half of what he desires, and he cannot sleep at all during the day because he is constantly passing waste from his body. The Luccan bath obviously imposed an ascetic regimen on its earnest visitors. Other spas had reputations for eating and drinking of near-banquet proportions, probably more a triumph of consumer demand than a rival theory of purgative medicine.

That Balthasar also had his doubts about the cure is made plain by his recurrent hope that "God will favor and protect" him until it is over; he is eager to be done with it and back at his business in Lucca. He finds, however, that the waters are treating him better than other patients. Some have come from a greater distance at greater effort and expense only to find the waters completely ineffectual and their stay indefinitely extended. "They drink it and it remains completely within them. . . . There are people here who would gladly give a hundred Italian crowns if the water would pass through them the way it does through me."

Balthasar spent twelve days at the Luccan springs, from June 21 to July 3. When he writes again to Mag-

dalena, on July 18, it is to share with her a new diagnosis by his physicians, "something I should not with-
hold from you." Although he otherwise feels fine, he
has a headache that will not relent.

Having reflected on
his condition, his physicians have concluded that he is
suffering from a "hot liver," which, while helped somewhat by the waters, has, in combination with his weak
stomach and poor digestion, produced "bad fumes" in
his head and inflamed his veins, thereby extending
weakness and pain into his extremities as well. Hence
his recurrent rheumatic pains and headaches. His physicians recommend that he return to the springs and
bathe both his head and his torso in the healing waters
for two hours each day over a period of at least six
weeks, while continuing to drink the water. To a modern
reader the diagnosis and prescription suggest enterprising business links between the springs and the Luccan
medical profession. Balthasar was not, however, so suspicious, and he did have a persistent headache. He would
have followed his physicians' recommendation had time
permitted (ten years later he will undergo just such a
prolonged cure), but the Frankfurt fair called him away.
He took the physicians' advice seriously and hoped to
pursue such treatment in Germany. Meanwhile, he tells
Magdalena that he is placing himself "in the hands of
the loving God, the best Physician and Healer, who is
best able to help me, according to his divine will."

The next time we find Balthasar at the baths, it is at
Carlsbad, in the northwestern corner of Bohemia. In
June 1591 he embarked on a more ambitious cure there,
one that in the end rivaled his rheumatic pains in un-
pleasantness. On the day of his arrival he rests, on the
second he purges (apparently by laxative), and on the
third he begins to "drink the waters every day." He
"purges quickly, but painlessly," feels good, and has his
fingers crossed that the travel, time, and money invested
in the cure will be justified. He again wants the cure

over as soon as possible, but he is completely unable to predict its length. He remains ready to depart at a word. His fear is that his stay will be prolonged, that "one day will stretch into ten." For the moment, he is "at the mercy of the doctor." He has obviously learned some lessons about dealing with the asceticism of the baths. Far more so than the Luccan springs, Carlsbad is described as a "truly miserly" place, where one can buy neither wine nor beer to help pass the time. However, Balthasar will not go hungry again. One Hans Köppel in nearby Schlackenwalde has provided him with a rabbit and a batch of chickens. His boarding problem having been solved in this way, Balthasar's chief complaint at present is an undependable servant, whose failure to make proper arrangements for the delivery of his trunks has left him without a change of clothes and virtually confined to quarters.

After a week of the cure, Balthasar reports to Magdalena that "there is no end to my dirty work." Having drunk over fourteen liters of the healing waters, he believes he has undergone as thorough a purging as one could desire. His doctor is now requiring him to bathe in the water twice a day for half an hour, on one of these occasions not above his navel, and to take head showers as well, a regimen he is to follow for eight to ten days. Because the cure is lasting so long and has taken so much out of him, Balthasar now expects he will be unable to ride at his normal pace and so he plans to rest at the homes of friends en route. This will mean arriving home later than planned.

A final letter, on June 20, brings news that he not only will be traveling more slowly because of the cure, but will also be departing Carlsbad at a later date because Providence has elected to interrupt his cure. "Know that just as my cure was almost completed, the Lord God assailed me with severe facial inflammation,

so that the entire left side of my face is terribly swollen"—possibly an ear infection induced by his head
showers. Because of the pain he now suffers, he must,
against his will, extend his stay at the bath until the
swelling goes down. He says he is patiently "awaiting
the improvement God will soon graciously send me,
according to his fatherly will." His faith in God, both
his Afflicter and his Redeemer, is now exceedingly great;
he claims improvement already, but so slight that one
can hardly detect it. That Balthasar could in the same
letter both blame God for spoiling his cure and trust
him to save him from it involved no contradiction on
his part; when medicine failed, as it so often did in the
sixteenth century, there was always and only God.

In June 1594, Balthasar began a long cure in Lucca
under the supervision of a new physician. This cure
would stretch over three months, both in Lucca and at
the springs, and would proceed very gradually. It began
with an array of mild laxatives, progressed to drinking
the waters, and ended with a near-month-long consecu-
tive stay at the springs. Balthasar writes excitedly about
his new physician, describing him as a "truly diligent
man, who very carefully observes and ponders my anat-
omy and all other matters." Balthasar clearly wants to
trust the doctor, but his experiences of the fallibility of
the medical profession restrain him. As faith is always
quick to surface in his mind when doubts about God
seem imminent, so skepticism is never far away when a
physician offers advice. In the struggle for minds in
early modern Europe, the physician fought an uphill
battle. "I must trust," Balthasar says of his new doctor,
"that he has not advised anything bad for me"—hardly
a faith to move mountains. Still, through the skill of his
physician, Balthasar expects the Luccan springs to do
him more good now than they did in the past, but only
"if God is willing."

The cure began with rest and reacclimation to Lucca,

as Balthasar had just returned from a week's business trip. Over a period of eleven days, he then ingested nine different medicinal syrups, beginning with a mild purgative known as *manna cabrina*, a mixture of juices from several medicinal plants that proved to be both pleasant and highly effective, and culminating in a special elixir that purged him thoroughly without any accompanying enfeeblement. All medicines were prescribed "in harmony with the reigning weather," which at the time was moist, cool, and windy. On five mornings Balthasar also drank the juice of two large lemons. Only then did he begin to drink water imported from the springs. According to his physician, the cure would work only if they proceeded slowly and conscientiously, with daily examinations of the waste being driven from his body. If the water agreed with him and he prospered from it, the physician planned to send him to the springs during the month of August. Balthasar's prescribed role in the cure at this point was to moderate his eating and drinking, and especially avoid overeating at night. "So far," he writes, "I find myself, praise and thank God, doing very well; may God continue to extend his blessing to me."

After three weeks Balthasar reports "good news." His physician has assured him that had he not undertaken the long cure, "the great filth that now passes so frequently from me and, as he says, is lodged around my liver, constraining and inflaming it, would have caused a serious illness before summer's end." He continues to take purgatives, but he has also been drinking the waters for five days with good results. "The waters have driven a great deal of filth from me, which my physician examines every morning. Today, to give me some rest, he suspended my drinking and in its place gave me an enema, which has also drawn a great deal of slime from me." Tomorrow all such purgations are to end and Balthasar will drink nothing but water from the springs, two and a half liters a day for three days. On June 27 he received his last herbal dose, a "manna" in meat broth that he says "really purged" him. If his business permits, he plans to spend the greater part of August at the springs, as the air is far healthier there at that time of the year than in Lucca, and there he thinks he can also escape the tedium of his work. Obviously the business world has become more predictably burdensome to him than the baths. Perhaps also, with the passage of years, Balthasar too, like the majority of Luccans who visited the springs, now hoped to derive a little pleasure from them.

His physician recommended at this point in his cure that he take walks during his leisure hours rather than write letters. Walking was the more relaxing and recuperative diversion, less likely to rile emotions and upset the humors. "Assuming I continue to follow his counsel in all matters, my physician is well satisfied with my progress, save that today, after a week's purging and after my enema, [he thinks] I should spend more of my time walking than writing even though I am doing well; he does not want letter day to work against me." Hence, an all too brief letter.

Magdalena followed every step of Balthasar's cure keenly, almost to the point of meddling. She instructs him to interrogate his physician about specific steps he can take to prevent the recurrence of his rheumatic pains. She is curious to know his opinion of Veronica water (speedwell) and lavender sugar, a mixture she takes daily in addition to rose sugar for her own health with good results. She thinks it can also help Balthasar. And what does the physician prescribe for head colds? She is prepared to send Veronica water immediately, if he so recommends. Magdalena's enthusiasm for contemporary medicine knows none of Balthasar's skeptical restraint, but then she seems never to have endured the regimen of a thermal bath. She describes the purgation through which he is going as "God's means of graciously preserving you," as if in his cure he was receiving God's special help as surely as when he took holy sacraments from the hands of a priest.

By mid-July the weeks of purging had left Balthasar dehydrated and "vexed with itching," a condition made worse by the intense summer heat. He struggles not to scratch. Still, he is happy that this is his only problem, although he suspects that it may force him to enter the waters earlier than he had planned, if a remedy for the itching is not quickly found. Magdalena had hoped that the purgative process in Lucca—the laxatives, the enemas, and drinking the water—would be cure enough. It distresses her to learn about his apparently early departure to the springs, since a stay there threatens to delay his journey home. "You will certainly have to stay that much longer at the springs [as well as go there earlier], for, unlike Carlsbad, one must remain at the Luccan springs until one is well again."

A simple, effective remedy was, however, found for Balthasar's itching: bathing daily for one hour in a scant pail of warmed spring water; so he did not enter the baths until around August 20. There he remained until at least mid-September. In his first letter to Magdalena after settling in, he reports having spent four days "drinking the waters and digesting and passing very well" everything out of him by midday when he rises for lunch. He anticipates continuing this routine (that is, merely drinking) for three to five more days before bathing in the springs for a week. During his visit to Carlsbad, in the summer of 1591, he had taken steps to mitigate its Spartan life by importing chickens. He now puts the ascetic regimen of the baths completely behind him. He has made the acquaintance of a Lucceser, a near relative of the Bishop of Lucca and a man accustomed to living well, with whom he drinks and dines at a nearby inn (he speaks even of "banqueting"). He still complains about the high cost of the spa, and he hopes to be done with the cure and back in Lucca within two weeks. Meanwhile, his servant Caspar travels back and forth to the city to fetch for him whatever he requires.

His chief regret this time is the absence of entertainment. The one amusement that saves him from mind-numbing boredom is high-stakes gambling wherein players lose sums up to five or six hundred Italian crowns in a single game, a sizable sum even for a wealthy man. Balthasar had neither the temperament nor the money to wager casually on such a scale; by both choice and necessity he remained a spectator, although he claims that he would have had no interest even in watching were it not for the boredom of the baths. Apparently many others should have followed his example. "There is no end to the sighing and complaining among those who lose," he writes. Prominent among them was his own roommate, a circumstance that must have made the contests all the more engrossing for Balthasar. His description of the man suggests a textbook compulsive gambler. Although he has yet to win a game, and on his first outing lost five hundred crowns, the man remains convinced that the cards will favor him and his losses will be recouped. Meanwhile, he can neither sleep nor eat until he has played. When they enter the dining hall for lunch, he thinks only of putting together a new game. "It is a great pity," Balthasar observes, "for he has six children. He forthrightly acknowledges that what he is doing is wrong and he knows he must stop, but he cannot hold himself back. He is also drinking the water, but it will do little for him in this regard." For Balthasar, the Luccan water cure remained gamble enough.

Balthasar ended his stay at the baths on a sour note. Following eleven days of purging and drinking the waters, he had spent at least a week bathing for two hours a day. Although he did all these things dutifully in the hope of "refreshing his liver," and he had not yet given up all hope of improvement, his pain had suddenly returned and he now feared he would never be completely rid of it. The main problem was again intestinal, ostensibly gastritis or ulcers, an ailment that had plagued him for years. In mid-September he departed the baths, accusing the waters of "not doing right by my stomach." "Brace yourself," he warns Magdalena, "to learn that the waters did not help my stomach, but instead brought pain to it, so that I soon gave them up and I have once again departed the bath. I have not been able to bathe away my inflammation, which now constantly torments me all too much." Despite the long cure, his health was now so poor and "constantly vexing," with both stomach and rheumatic pains, that he contemplated canceling a business trip to Genoa.

But Balthasar was back at the baths two years later, in April 1596, this time at the pastoral German spa in Langenschwalbach, in the vicinity of Mainz, with its cold, iron-laden mineral springs. There we find him again "in God's name . . . drinking, peeing, walking, and sweating a lot," and especially "trusting God" to make the good effects of the cure stay with him. God has become prominent in his thoughts as his doubts about the cure have increased. He believes that the waters of Langenschwalbach may do him good, however, if the cold springs there do not "chill" his stomach. He again hopes a week will be enough. The weather is cooperating. "If the waters don't help this time," he assures Magdalena, "it will not be the fault of the weather." The accommodations are superior to those of Carlsbad, and Langenschwalbach also has many delightful meadow, forest, mountain, and valley walks. But things do not start off well. He drank too much at first, and now he may only "sip" the waters. His roommate, a well-to-do physician who is also taking the cure, rarely hikes with him despite a desire to do so, because "everything he drinks stays in him and stops him up" so that he remains bedridden most of the time. Will Balthasar be next? The odds, he knew all too well, did not favor success.

We do not find Balthasar at the baths again in the correspondence, although this is no reason to believe that he never returned before his death in 1600. The spectacle of a physician betrayed by the waters may have given him true pause. In light of his own sad experiences, he may even in his more skeptical moments have looked on the physician's suffering as poetic justice. More likely, though, the physician's faith in the cure and his persistence in it even when it seemed to strike him down reassured Balthasar. The alternatives to the cure were at least as discouraging. Without the cure, there was, in the end, only God to care for one's health, and God's record was also none too good. The cure, after all, consisted as much in the chase as in the catch. It allowed Balthasar to be active on his own behalf, to do something tangible for his health, to ponder and exchange information with physicians, to experiment with new medicines and procedures. Even if it did not in the end work, it also never left a person simply resigned. The rule of sixteenth-century medicine was, try and try again; the best cure was always the next cure.

*VI*

# ℬELIEVERS

Nuremberg in the time of Magdalena and Balthasar was officially Lutheran. The magistrates had banned all Catholic clergy and public Catholic services after the triumph of the Reformation there in 1525. During the second half of the century, a sizable minority within the city held Reformed, or Calvinist, beliefs. Staunchly Lutheran territories and local critics who subscribed to the Formula of Concord (1577), a triumph of conservative Lutheran doctrine, considered Nuremberg to be too liberally Lutheran, even crypto-Calvinist. Although Nuremberg did not join the larger Lutheran world in embracing the Formula of Concord, the magistrates effectively dispelled any fears among their Lutheran allies that the city might drift into Calvinism. In the 1580s, for example they quashed efforts by a colony of Netherlands clothmakers, whose religious predilections were Calvinist, to boycott the sacrament of baptism in the city's churches because of the Lutheran rite of exorcism that accompanied it. Believing that all unbaptized infants, born as they were in original sin, were possessed by the Devil, Lutherans "exorcised" them as a prelude to their baptism. Calvinists found the rite offensive, too traditional and in conflict with their belief that God had predestined each soul from eternity.

The magistrates' firm resolve to steer a middle course between liberal and conservative Lutherans allowed a spectrum of Protestant opinion to flourish among the city's clergy and intellectuals. The magistrates also had to manage the city's continuing political obligations to the Catholic emperor while at the same time respecting the Protestant beliefs of the majority of its citizenry—no small feat for perhaps the leading Lutheran city in the Empire. This balancing act was expertly accomplished. Only for a brief period in 1548, after a short-lived imperial victory over the Protestant princes, did the Mass reappear in the city. When Emperor Ferdinand I visited the city in 1559 and requested a celebration of the Mass, the magistrates, true to the Reformation, firmly refused him. Still, a few "neutralized" Catholic institutions persisted in the city throughout the sixteenth century under careful magisterial supervision. The Order of the Knights of St. John, a lay military order devoted to the Virgin that had existed in the city since the thirteenth century, survived the Reformation as an aristocratic enclave of traditional piety. A few monasteries and nunneries also continued after the Reformation, permitted to exist so long as their members freely chose to live within their walls. Although the taking in of new members was forbidden, exceptions were occasionally made. The city's Dominican monastery persisted until 1543, the Cistercian cloister until 1562, and the convents of St. Clara and St. Katherine until 1596, when their last surviving members died. The religious in these cloisters privately celebrated the Mass, and local laity who continued to desire traditional rites reportedly joined them covertly and illegally.

In 1593 the papal secretary for German affairs criticized Nuremberg's treatment of resident Italian Catholic merchants, who had become an important part of the city's business community and cultural life. Particularly resented was the magistrates' refusal to permit an Italian priest to reside in the city for the purpose of hearing confessions and celebrating the Mass. Nuremberg Catholics could practice their religion publicly and legally only by traveling to neighboring Catholic territories. Some Nuremberg families made regular contributions toward the support of an Italian priest in nearby Buchenbach bei Erlangen, in the bishopric of Bamberg, in order to ensure regular Catholic services at a manageable distance from the city. Cloisters in the neighboring diocese of Eichstatt provided still another opportunity, and Nuremberg merchants who regularly attended the Frankfurt fairs could receive the sacraments there. Within Nuremberg, however, save for the inmates of cloisters, Catholic services remained strictly forbidden.

In 1598 Pope Clement VIII issued a bull threatening to excommunicate any Catholic who resided in Nuremberg without papal dispensation, an apparent effort to exact a few concessions from the magistrates by threatening the city's lucrative Italian trade. The threat proved to be of little consequence, as the specter of disrupted trade with the city clearly set Catholic merchants as much atremble as did the prospect of a breach with the Pope. Nuremberg remained a great Protestant city, and Italian Catholic merchants continued to flourish there.

# ❧THE SOVEREIGNTY OF GOD

BALTHASAR TO MAGDALENA
*9 November 1591, in Lucca*

Honest and kind, dear Magdalena:
    Not a little do I desire to hear of your well-being and that of all those who are ours. I thank Almighty God that I am well. I wrote you most recently on November 6 to announce my safe arrival here, and as I have since

Dum ngris egrum prope Mors circumuolat alis,     Tum me promißis beat et domus omnis ailorat,
  Funestamq; aciem iam fera iamq; parat.    Ο ΘΕΟΣ .     Tum vocat immensum me veneratat DEVM

The figure of Christ as a physician, seen here in an engraving by the Dutch artist Hendrick Goltzius, circa 1587, reflects
the Nuremberg physicians' view of their profession as di-
vinely inspired. In his right hand Christ holds a urinal and
in his left a porcelain container of salve. Around his waist
hangs surgical cutlery, while at his feet lie various medical
books and devices. In the background the sick are nursed
and operations are in progress. The verses spoken by Christ
read:

When Death with his black wings hovers over the sick man,
    And makes ready his funereal array and scythe,
Then does the sick man delight me with his vows of faith
        and the entire house beseech me,
    And having thus supplicated me, he calls upon the
        measureless power of God.

received no letter from you, I have all the less to write you in this letter. This letter is made possible only because of the good opportunity provided by cousin Hans Christoph Scheurl, who departs [for home] today in God's name. May our Lord God at all times be his gracious escort! I could not arrange to visit you with him.

I arrived here just in the nick of time, while the weather was still good. On the very day of my arrival, as soon as I had dismounted from my horse, it began to rain, and it has done little else since. This is the way the weather always is here in the wintertime. So it is tedious enough for me, but I must apply myself, as I am still settling in. It is strange to be here now because I am so completely out of the habit [of living in Lucca]. I must get to know the people here all over again, because during the 7 or 7½ years since I was last here, much has changed. In the end everything must be put in order; as I have begun, so, God willing, will I carry forward and complete it.

Our maid here is very pleased to have gained a servant in Hans, whom I have made keeper of the cellar. She orders him to do one thing after the other. He already has to help her make the beds, and she talks to him as if he understood the language. In this way he will soon learn it (for he also enjoys this).

In this land there is still everywhere very great famine. The wheat that our people here bought to make bread for the house at 25 to 26 gulden per Nuremberg gross bushel during the harvest is now selling at 27 to 28 gulden. One estimates that a year from now one-third of the people in the whole of Italy may be dead. If it does not happen [on this magnitude], it will still happen, because for so many there is simply nothing to eat. They must die of hunger; even if a third of the population does not die, many must still starve to death. That such a great famine exists throughout the whole of Italy is an obvious punishment of God. Time offers little hope of improvement, especially in Sicily. Not only throughout Italy, but also in a good part of Spain where people also feed themselves with grain, the famine and starvation are greatest where the people cannot forgo the seed grain that otherwise should be planted, but now must be used for daily nourishment—which only portends future suffering, since what one does not sow, one also cannot harvest. Here, on the land, is just now the greatest seed time, which the [premature] onset of rainy weather, should it continue, will harm. So it does not at all appear that people may soon count on any cheap grain. May our Lord God have mercy on the poor and send soon a gracious improvement! Amen.

A year ago, the carpenter who made the walnut chair and table for me also bought a walnut tree for me and left it off at a sawmill to be cut. He has subsequently told me that he does not understand why the tree could not be cut there [but it has not been]. So I have sent for it and instructed that it be done at another mill in the vicinity of Wöhrd.

I would like you to tell little Balthasar to be very good and study diligently, otherwise we will not be friends and I will bring him nothing.

I do not know anything more to write you, kind, dear Magdel, only to ask you to greet warmly on my behalf Conrad Bair, brother-in-law Stephan Bair, my sisters, Frau Paul Scheurl, Frau Christoph Gröser, brother-in-law Hans Christoph von Plauen and his wife—in sum, all our good friends and acquaintances, who are in my best thoughts. And many friendly and warm greetings to you and to our household. May we all be kept in the grace of our Lord God.

> *Your loyal, loving, husband,*
> *Balthasar Paumgartner the Younger*

Balthasar and Magdalena barely comment on matters of institutional religion. High theology and church politics were not their preserve and were left to the clergy and the magistrates. What little they do say about church policy, however, suggests that they did not find Nuremberg's ecclesiastical governance intimidating or even constraining, nor were they in any overt way anti-clerical. Whether Balthasar was in Nuremberg or in Italy, he freely and unself-consciously mingled with Italian Catholic merchants, three of whom he mentions by name in his letters and with obvious respect. One, Torisani, whose firm was based in Florence, may even have been a friend. Resident in Nuremberg since 1570, he or members of his firm several times advised and assisted Balthasar and Magdalena. They helped them find windows for their house, lent Balthasar horses, and provided cousin Paul Scheurl with coach transportation to Frankfurt, in addition to other business-related favors and services, which Balthasar repaid in kind. In the everyday life of the merchant, religious allegiance and practice appear to have been taken very much in stride. When Pope Innocent IX died, in December 1591 while Balthasar was in Lucca, Balthasar, without giving the matter a second thought, did as the Luccans and fasted for two days prior to the celebration of the new Pope. He reports that he had already "served [the Pope] well" in this regard for over twenty-four hours, but he admits to uncertainty about how his servant Hans is taking the fasting (whether this is because Hans was of strong Protestant sentiment or simply liked to eat is left unclear). Balthasar also claims that the period of fasting has permitted him "to get all the more writing done," a boon to his business correspondence. Obviously, he did not spend the time in pious meditation.

Magdalena's few direct comments on institutional religion suggest independence, sympathy, and even a sense of humor. On one occasion she observes that cousin Paul Scheurl had at one time wanted all the Calvinists dead, whereas now he goes so far as to "flatter" one of them. The person she had in mind was Anthony Geuder, one of the powerful thirteen senior burgomasters, a man very prominent in setting the city's religious policy.

Magdalena's comment was occasioned by her annoyance at Scheurl for having given Geuder two barrels of a rare wine she had herself begged him for. In the world around Magdalena and Balthasar, a pragmatic peace, built up from close personal contact and material self-interest, reigned among the ordinary practitioners of the city's religious confessions, whether Lutheran, Calvinist, or Catholic.

Magdalena could joke, at times almost bawdily, about other matters of institutional religion. Alluding to the clergy's ban on dancing in the city, in reaction to Turkish victories in eastern Europe (the clergy routinely designed such penances in times of crisis, as civic petitions for providential favor), she describes the Schmitmers' tedious engagement party at which she claims "the people contrived for so long and the men got so drunk that I thought it would not have been much of a sin [by comparison] had they danced before." Magdalena's comment may be seen as a biting one when one remembers her own fondness for dancing. On another occasion she reports the imminent burial of Frau Martin Haller, who had died after a long bout with dysentery. Magdalena learned from others that during the last weeks of her life, when she was apparently frequently at church, she had been unable to control her bowels. "Her bowels moved in church whenever she began to laugh; [people say] that was something she got without having to pay the church for it." Either Frau Haller was a woman perceived as trying to buy her way into heaven or Magdalena here shares a mildly anticlerical sentiment.

If the institutional side of religion is not prominent in Magdalena's and Balthasar's correspondence, the personal side of religion most definitely is. They are true believers who constantly find God at the boundary between success and failure, sickness and health, life and death—and they hold him responsible for all. For them,

God is the only spiritual power in the world, the sole supernatural force freely at work in the universe. Never in the correspondence do they so much as mention competing supernatural powers—although witches and demons were subjects of popular interest and were occasionally commented on in public sermons and pamphlets. Their own misfortunes, events in their lives that remain beyond their comprehension and control— whether a failed cure, a lost business deal, or the death of an only child—are interpreted as God's "seizing upon" and "afflicting" them. They think of God as an absolutely omnipotent being, who controls human destiny on earth and into eternity, justly, for good and for ill, in accordance with his own unfathomable will. When famine strikes Italy in 1591, threatening to kill one-third of the population, or when drought devastates Spain, Balthasar knows both the reason and the source: God is punishing manifest sins in both lands. When the vineyards fail in Germany, Italy, and France in 1596, and the poorest harvest in twelve years yields only expensive and sour wine, Balthasar, a confessed drinker, declares it to be "an obvious punishment of God; it happens because of our sins, because people abuse wine so outrageously." When the pain of a urinary-tract infection leaves Frau Behaim crying day and night and her physicians can provide no relief, Magdalena believes the explanation must in part be that "she is being punished [by God] for her untrue heart," a reference to an unspecified, but to Magdalena well-known, moral failing.

Balthasar and Magdalena regularly commend deceased friends and acquaintances to God. Those for whom they have uncommon affection they commend repeatedly. "May the Almighty be to him as to all of us gracious and merciful and grant him after this life eternal life!" Balthasar writes when Sebastian Imhoff, a merchant friend, dies in Lyon. "May the eternal good God grant both of them and all of us a happy resurrection," he

writes on the occasion of the deaths of his Aunt Nützel
and Frau Georg Volckamer. On three separate occasions
Balthasar wishes his dear deceased friend Conrad Bair
"God's grace and mercy and a happy resurrection in
Christ." When Magdalena sends news of the death of
Aunt Nützel, she is pleased also to report that the
woman died "gladly and properly, praying only for salvation;" Magdalena trusts God will grant her the "happy
resurrection" her life on earth seems to deserve.

Such formulaic wishes abound in the correspondence,
as they acknowledge the fragility of humankind, the
clearest and most uncontestable fact of life for people in early modern Europe. Balthasar and Magdalena
reflect often and profoundly on this; for them, its recognition is the beginning of religion. Pondering the passing of so many friends of their youth, Balthasar confides: "In sum, there is nothing lasting in our world.
That is why we should reasonably build much more
upon what is eternal than upon what is temporal. May
eternal God be gracious and merciful to our friends and
to us all and grant us eternal happiness when our frail
lives have ended." On another occasion Balthasar allows
himself to dwell on the death of his dear Aunt Nützel
and to remember how she had been a trusted adviser
and generous friend since his youth. Suddenly, he breaks
off his revery, catching himself with a sharp reminder of
a fundamental truth: "In this world one must nevertheless not stake one's life on human help"—which Balthasar knew all too well might be present today but not
tomorrow, might work one day but not the next.

Magdalena and Balthasar believed God to be good
and merciful as well as omnipotent and free, a being
who acted independently without being asked, and who
also responded directly to prayer and entreaty. We find
them alternately beseeching God for some special assistance they desire and thanking him for some protective
act they believe he has, unsolicited and unmerited on

their part, bestowed on them. Magdalena prays daily for Balthasar when he travels, convinced that "God, who has already brought Balthasar safely through so much, will with his dear angels do so still again." When Balthasar begins his first cure at the Luccan springs, she hopes that "Almighty God will grant my heartfelt prayers and restore your health there by Christian means, since it has not been his will to do so here [in Nuremberg]. May God preserve you at all times and bring you safely back to me in joy . . ." Magdalena's ability to describe the springs as a "Christian means" of healing is a commentary on her faith in contemporary purgative medicine. Enemas, bleeding cups, and sulphuric waters are for her as much a part of the divine arsenal against physical evil as are the Bible and prayers, and she believes their neglect to be just as ominous for one's well-being.

The more hopeless a situation is, the more abjectly do Magdalena and Balthasar rely on God. As Magdalena sat by the bedside of old Frau Behaim, watching her agonize beyond relief for two successive nights "because the water in her had become inflamed," she begged God to "help her [Frau Behaim] survive the pain and to deliver us from ever knowing such pain." The same prayerful empathy was extended to the Roggenbachs' sister's child as he lay dying from gangrene. And as old Bair's diseased body rotted away before Magdalena's eyes and he reached the point where he could no longer recognize her face, she urged the Lord God to "end it soon" for him.

The world of Balthasar and Magdalena was one in which security or calamity always remained one gratuitous divine decision away. "We are today sitting in the rose garden," she writes Balthasar on a pleasant day in January 1592, "safe from the famine you are now having in Italy. What a pitiable life it must be when the people are dying so from hunger! May God mercifully protect us from such a calamity." In the same religious vein, Balthasar likes to commend his own health to the hands of the "divine Physician." In light of his own medical history, he must have done so as much out of despera- tion as in any hope. "I leave my ailing stomach and head to the loving God," he writes from Lucca at the end of his first cure; "he is able to mend both, according to his divine will." When a "great pain" suddenly recedes from his teeth, God gets the credit.

Perhaps because he viewed the world through the eyes of a merchant, Balthasar could think of God as a clever operator when he chose to intervene in the affairs of men and confound Balthasar's enemies. Explaining his father's ability on more than one occasion to recover his failing health when all seemed lost for him, Baltha- sar invokes divine cunning. "I believe that our Lord God has granted it to my father to outlive those who would like to see him dead, so that they [his father's political foes in Altdorf] will have to deal with him that much longer."

Magdalena and Balthasar doubted neither God's power nor his goodness. Theirs was a God who never left peo- ple without hope. On the other hand, one could never be sure of his will and pleasure. Although able to relieve any pain and remedy any ill, God manifestly did not always do so. What he deemed good in the mystery of his will was often not experienced as such by his crea- tures, who had nonetheless to accept and bear it. Mag- dalena and Balthasar choose the only reasonable course of action in a world controlled by such a deity: they hope for the best outcome when misfortune strikes, while preparing to endure the worst. Balthasar's com- ments on the death of his son define precisely the am- bivalent situation they found themselves in before God. Learning from Magdalena that little Balthasar's death was imminent, Balthasar informed her. of his plans to depart immediately for home. He did not know that as he wrote little Balthasar was already dead. He assesses their plight:

Unless the almighty, good God and father should now grant us his special grace and help, any further human effort [by the physicians] will be in vain. He [God] is the highest and best Physician, who, when he chooses, can indeed help. Therefore, so long as there is breath in little Balthasar, I still have hope, although small, that our Lord God will once more act for the best, according to his gracious, fatherly will, to which we all should reasonably surrender ourselves.

Magdalena and Balthasar of course interpret God in terms of their own experience. But their understanding of deity seems also to have been shaped by the teaching of Nuremberg's pastors. The sovereignty of God over world affairs was a fundamental tenet of the Lutheran clergy. In 1590 the city of Weissenburg requested through Nuremberg's magistrates the clergy's opinion of the power of witches and how best to deal with them. The Weissenburgers sought such instruction at this time because popular interest in magic and witchcraft was on the rise and official persecution of witches under way in parts of Franconia. The request became an occasion for the clergy to expound on the sovereignty of God. They dutifully conveyed their opinion to the magistrates, who in turn passed it on to their counterparts in Weissenburg.

The instruction circulated only privately at this time. In 1613 it first appeared as a popular pamphlet under the title "A Thorough Report on How to Deal with Magic and Witchcraft: A Clear Answer From the Learned Theologians and Preachers of Nuremberg," and it bore the signatures of Nuremberg's church superintendent and the pastors of its five churches. The "Report" exemplifies the popular theology on the subject that was preached to laity like Magdalena and Balthasar.

It deems witchcraft a largely involuntary delusion afflicting people who are simple-minded, ignorant, melancholy, impoverished, and/or ill. For all save the most extreme cases the clergy recommend treatments and penalties well short of death. Their overriding concern is to contradict the notion that Satan and his witches have independent magical powers to work evil in the world at will. According to the pastors, God is the singular, uncontested force behind all worldly events regardless of their outcome.

> Whatever Satan does in the world, God has preordained that he do it. . . . Satan's acts have nothing to do with any power of his own, but occur only at the behest of God. Satan cannot boast of his works, as if he had done them by his own power, as if he himself were able to propose and dispose at will without God's permission. The same is true of the foul magic of witches. When they claim to have done harm to people, cattle, and other creatures by causing storms and fires, it is pure blindness and delusion on their part. The ability to do such works is not even in the Devil's power and will, much less in theirs.

Thus did Nuremberg's clergy scoff at the notion that Satan and his followers had free run of the world. They cite the very persistence of life and the evidence of so much good fortune as positive proof of God's restraint of his wrath and circumscription of Satan's destructiveness. Despite appearances, "it is God who makes everything happen, and for the best."

This message Magdalena and Balthasar had long absorbed. The only mention made of the Devil in the correspondence is Magdalena's quotation of her ne'er-do-well brother-in-law Caspar's exclamation "May the Devil take me," on one of the many occasions when Caspar tried to persuade his relatives that he could be trusted to keep his word. Neither Magdalena nor Baltha-

sar ever makes independent mention of the Devil, and
if they believed in witchcraft and magic they also never
comment on them. For them, God alone manages world
affairs. Their one overriding religious concern is that he
conduct these affairs charitably, so that the results may
prove as pleasing to them as they presumably are to
him.

That God responded to prayer and penance was also a
basic tenet of the popular theology preached to the laity
by Nuremberg's clergy. This can be seen especially during the 1590s, when Turkish armies threatened to over-
run Hungary and invade western Europe. The clergy in
these years arranged special services to gain divine in-
tervention on the West's behalf. Among the measures
taken in Nuremberg churches were new Sunday sermons and extended, citywide weekday prayer vigils (a
quarter hour, double the normal period of time). Magdalena, a beehive of war news, documents the city's
pervasive fear and unrest. Her letters keep Balthasar
abreast of the comings and goings of princes and troops
as they muster in Nuremberg en route to the Turkish
front. There are vivid descriptions of the training of
draftees, who, outfitted in red-and-white jackets, spiked
helmets, and muskets, keep the city astir as they practice on paper targets at the ends of city streets and occasionally on migrating geese. Nothing terrified Magdalena more than the thought of Turkish rule; "better a
plague than the Turk," she tells Balthasar.

Magdalena did not, however, require such extraordinary historical events to turn her mind to God. She
seems to have read the Bible. In 1588 she asks Balthasar
to buy an "Old Testament with the Psalms and the
Prophets, for we often need it." Among the goods he
shipped to her for distribution in 1596 was a German
Bible. She invokes a Biblical allusion to describe preparations for war against the Turks: "Now is truly that
very time when the Lord Christ says one will hear of

war and cries of war." When bad news arrives from the war zone she is immediately among the prayerful. "We have every reason to pray constantly," she urges; "may God be merciful and in his time help us for the sake of the small children." Learning, she claims without surprise, that the princes and lords who attended a recent Imperial Diet in Nuremberg convened by the Emperor to raise fresh troops for the eastern front did nothing but eat and drink—"the princes pledged themselves to one another with nightcaps, like stablehands"—she allows that "God must now come and take charge; may he graciously help us so that the innocent do not suffer along with the guilty."

Despite their frequent petitions for divine aid, neither Magdalena nor Balthasar considered prayer and penance sure means of securing divine favor. Such acts, as Balthasar put it, were simply a "reasonable" recognition of divine sovereignty over life's boundaries. The pair had watched too many "innocent" relatives and friends suffer and die, despite their prayers, to have believed otherwise. No matter what mortals do, whether on their knees or on their feet, they remain at God's mercy; of that Magdalena and Balthasar had no doubt.

## ❧ SELF-RELIANCE

MAGDALENA TO BALTHASAR
*13 September 1592, in Nuremberg*

Honest, kind, dearest Paumgartner:
Your letter reached me last Saturday, and I was joyed to learn of your safe arrival [in Frankfurt] and that there is now much work for you there. May God grant that all goes well and that your work may be promptly finished, so that we may come together again in joy—

although God has now made a painful tear through our joy.* In the past we have always been able to reunite with greater happiness than will unfortunately happen now. Nevertheless, our strong hope in God can again make us joyful. Amen.

Dear Paumgartner, I have read with pleasure all the news in your letter, [and I have] also [learned] that the quinces are not a success. Nevertheless, would you try to get at least 300 for us, if you cannot get more? If you have also inquired about golden pears for yourself, you have done well. When you depart, buy some knives for the servants and simple folk. And do not forget sugar.

I have today written to old Frau Köppel in Schlackenwalde to remind her not to forget about the flax; I sent along a dozen honeycakes to make it easier for her to remember.

Herr [Hieronymus] Kress has today gained another son. They now have five sons. They could well give one to us, if it were permitted. Finold lifted him from the baptismal waters.† His name is Joachim Friedrich. I have just been to the baptism.

Early tomorrow I am going with Christoph to run his bird traps.

I must share with you some real news about the weather here. For the last three days, praise God, we have had good weather; since your departure the weather had been constantly rainy. Had the rain lasted any longer, it would soon have incited something.‡ For whenever it has rained around here, the rains have been torrential.

I also heard today that people are beginning to die there [in Italy, from plague]. Therefore, I ask you, dearest treasure, to take care of yourself and not to travel without first having eaten something.

During the past week, I have also worried about your father, who has not been well. But, praise God, we

* The death of little Balthasar.
† That is, he was the godfather.
‡ Disease and plague, as well as flooding, were associated with incessant rainfall.

have today received word that he is again a little better. I regret that you are not here and that we cannot go and be with him, because the end is now surely approaching. At this very moment, when I want only to write to you, a barrel of wine has arrived. And, as it is being put away, a letter from you has also just come, making me very happy. You will surely also by now have received my last letter. The barrel of wine that has just arrived contains almost 4 kegs [360 liters].

Since your departure, I have heard nothing from Adam Stutzer [about the horses], and he has not been at home. Perhaps the order [for the horses] has not yet come from Salzburg; therefore, I cannot well advise you to buy the horses [you desire in Frankfurt]. Should you bring the four horses [the two older browns and two new grays] together, a buyer may want to pay you that much less for the two browns. But it is your decision to make, and what pleases you also pleases me.

Dear Paumgartner, I also asked you in my first letter to get me 2 or 3 measures of linen—[at least] I believe I remembered to do so. You can get it for around 10 or 12 pazen a measure; I need it for a jerkin.

Dear love, I have at this time nothing more to write, except to report that our largest catch of birds on Sunday was 15. Today at 6:00 it began again to rain. May God give us good weather again soon!

Warm and sincere greetings, dearest Paumgartner; may the Lord God keep you in his grace.

*Magdalena Balthasar Paumgartner*


The unreliability of divine aid did not make Magdalena and Balthasar skeptics and anticlerics. Their personal experience of the "sovereignty of God" confirmed for them what their clergy had also taught: God may be implored, but he cannot be manipulated; he is all-powerful and free on the one hand, good and merciful on the other, and his daily rule on earth remains completely unpredictable—at times surprisingly beneficial, at times alarmingly disappointing.

A modern reader might suspect that a religion devoted to such a deity would inhibit action and foster desperation. To the contrary, Magdalena and Balthasar drew from it fresh resolve and initiative, new strength and independence. They shaped their own lives in the image of their ever-resourceful Maker. While they believed in God and attempted to live by his rules, they did not wait solely upon him for their health and wellbeing. As far as they were concerned, they had his leave to take charge of their lives, to act freely and shrewdly in their own behalf, to be bled and to bathe and to make money. Accordingly, they made the most of all their resources, whether cures, merchandise, or prayer. In doing so, they took care to be as reverent as they were enterprising. The imagination and the energy for their undertakings were self-consciously their own, but God invariably got the credit for the outcome in recognition of his sovereignty over life—praise when they succeeded, and blame when they failed or succumbed to misfortune. In the end, God infallibly disposed all things; but until he acted, Magdalena and Balthasar believed their lives to be very much their own proposing.

Balthasar reveals this during his first separation from Magdalena after their marriage, making clear the degree to which self-reliance characterized both their marital and their religious behavior. Magdalena had written to him of her successful coping with many personal and business affairs during his absence. Such diligence delighted Balthasar, who expected nothing less. In praising her abilities, he drew a parallel between her relationships to God and to him. "May the almighty, eternal God grant and impart to us all his grace, luck, blessing, and support. Meanwhile, take care of yourself and do nothing to give offense. As I would provide for you, provide also for yourself." Balthasar here instructs Magdalena to

trust God and her husband and in their absence to behave in such a way as to be pleasing to both; she is expected to run her own life, and as capably as any man.
When God and Balthasar *are* present, or when either
chooses to intervene in her life, it is assumed that they
will "provide" for her according to the freedom and
goodness of their respective wills. But Magdalena receives such attention as a free partner within a relationship, not as an object lacking effective agency or self-
direction.

Magdalena's most deeply held beliefs find expression
in revealing proverbs. One of her favorites is "Something must always go awry." She will say this when little Balthasar falls ill during his father's absence or when
she learns that Balthasar must travel with an ailing
horse. She thus acknowledges the most common characteristic of their lives: unpredictability and precariousness.
This was something she and Balthasar also recognized
as God's freedom and sovereignty over the world. Whatever happened, whether pain or pleasure, they were
quick to accept philosophically as an expression of divine will. For them, God and the world remained full of
surprises. Although always destabilizing and often dis-
maying, such interruptions, even when they resulted in
tragedy, never defeated or rendered them fatalistic.
Magdalena, especially, rebounds quickly from misfortune.

The same proverb surfaces on the occasion of a moral
dilemma Magdalena several times faced. In the fall of
1591, cousin Paul Scheurl persuaded her to provide
lodging and care for one of his relatives by marriage,
Frau Tobias Kastner of Engelthal, who was dying of
consumption. "Something must always go awry," she
writes Balthasar, as she shares with him her second
thoughts about having agreed to the arrangement.
Awaiting her arrival for a planned two-week stay, during which Frau Kastner's doctor was to see whether

anything could be done to reverse her decline, Magdalena worried that there was little hope of recovery and that she, Magdalena, would in all probability end up nursing the woman through a slow, lingering death. "Should God choose to afflict her for a long time," she complains to Balthasar, "she will cause me grief . . . I worry only that it is too late [for her to be helped]; as you know, she has been the same for a long time." As it turned out, Frau Kastner did revive while still in Engelthal, so that Magdalena did not have to nurse her in Nuremberg. When, at a later date, she came to Nuremberg to receive medical treatment, she stayed with her mother in another home, possibly because Magdalena had in the end frankly spoken of her reluctance to take Frau Kastner in.

This was not the only time Magdalena expressed reluctance to become involved. In December 1591, a Frau Stieber from the village of Ermreut visited her. Frau Stieber was at the time shopping in Nuremberg with her brothers and living at the home of the widow Schmidhammer. The party had brought their own food with them and were apparently counting their pennies. Visiting Magdalena, Frau Stieber complained that her lodging was entirely too expensive, and she seemed to be hinting that Magdalena should take her in out of charity. Magdalena, however, pretended not to understand, because, as she explained to Balthasar, a courteous invitation, which was appropriate under the circumstances, might have been accepted, and for an indefinite period of time. "I worried that she would take me seriously [if I invited her to stay]. I know well that hospitality should readily be extended to people, but there are too many in the household. She [Frau Stieber] sent for me to come to her today, but I told her I could not do so because I had to take care of a dying man, which is true." The dying man was Conrad Bair, whom she did indeed attend, but not so frequently or so exclusively as to have been rendered incapable of visiting Frau Stieber, had she at this time wished to pursue the relationship. Later in the new year when Frau Stieber returned to Nuremberg for Paul Behaim's wedding, Paul "quartered" her, at her request, with his sister. Magdalena writes Balthasar in mid-January 1592 that "the carpenter is raising the footboard and straightening the headboard of the walnut bed because I must put Frau Stieber there"; she asks Balthasar to send some green taffeta for a new bed curtain, if he thinks there should be one on the bed. Thus was the cold hand of hospitality extended!

Neither Magdalena nor Balthasar was really selfish. Spontaneous generosity and loyalty to relatives and friends run through their letters. When, four months before her marriage to Balthasar, Magdalena received gifts of food from Balthasar's father and stepmother, she immediately threw a feast with "all kinds of fun and games," inviting many friends and relatives. On another occasion, she reports "catching twenty-three large fowl" (actually from the nets of her brothers), which she directly shared with Jakob Imhoff's family. Balthasar once defined the rationale of generosity to relatives and friends when he agreed to assist the negotiations for the marriage of brother-in-law Paul Behaim to cousin Rosina Paumgartner. "In such established friendships as mine with Paul one should on special occasions hold all the more closely together and advise and help each other in every way one can." Charity and assistance were implicit in relationships, and the deeper the relationship, the more readily forthcoming they should be.

While Magdalena's services to relatives and friends were many, and she gives every indication of having had a guilty conscience when she could not go the extra mile, her charitable acts would on occasion be undertaken reluctantly. When charity threatened to become burdensome or to create relationships of near-total dependence, as in the case of Frau Kastner, Magdalena preferred to avoid contact altogether. She hesitates to embrace those who are not basically self-reliant, for such people leave her uneasy. She will assist but not manage the lives of others; she prefers to lend a hand, but does not want to become the hands. There may be some Lutheran influence here. Lutheran cities, with both civic and clerical support, legislated against religious mendicants and itinerant beggars, the nonlocal, "professionally" poor, whose growing numbers and presumption upon the charity of strangers had long concerned city councils. Lutheran tracts in the 1520s praised the needy who accepted aid only grudgingly and expressed eagerness to support themselves as soon as they were able. Nuremberg's welfare ordinance of 1522 prescribed both need and morals tests; successful applicants wore identifying badges. In the new Protestant regime, charity was viewed as more a governmental than an individual responsibility. The city restricted ongoing aid to the local poor, who received free food, medicine, and physician's care. Hard-hit local artisans might borrow up to 100 gulden in interest-free loans to keep their businesses going. The welfare budget for aid and services to the poor in 1586–87 exceeded 16,000 gulden, including payment of fees for bathing in healing springs off the island of Schütt. In 1574, the official count of the sick and needy was 700 chronic beggars and 2,540 "leprous" or diseased, figures that also included outsiders given temporary aid as they passed through the region. Probably 10 percent of the population received some regular care, while another 20 percent lived so marginal an existence that they, too, quickly became dependent on the city in periods of famine, plague, or war. William Smith, an impartial observer of Nuremberg's welfare system, found the city well prepared to dispense services. He praises its "many alms houses and . . . New Hospital" where weekly support was provided the poor and needy, "for none may be suffered to beg within the city, neither old nor young." The only exceptions he found were destitute orphaned children, who, following tradition, continued to circulate bread baskets and alms boxes on the streets three times a week while singing psalms.

If Magdalena and Balthasar associated life's uncertainty with divine sovereignty over the world, they also believed in an ultimate divine justice, a final and fair balancing of life's accounts. "In time, each will get what he deserves," is another of Magdalena's proverbs. She consoled Balthasar with it during the Frankfurt spring fair in 1597, when he was doubly afflicted, his body by intestinal distress and rheumatic pains, his peace of mind and profits by the Imperial Coinage Commission under Dr. Hüls. "I gather from your last letter that inflammation plagues you from within while the useless Dr. Hüls plagues all [the merchants] from without. He will someday get the reward he deserves."

Magdalena's basic nature was optimistic. "No matter how small something may be, it still has its promise." That proverbial consolation she offered to her brother-in-law Paul Paumgartner when he was casting about for a position with a merchant firm. Unemployed and restless, Paul had applied to several firms, including the Welsers, but he was particular and easily disspirited ("his desire sours") when obstacles appeared. As he anxiously awaited a decision, Magdalena assured him that anything might happen, and just as likely for the best as for the worst. The sentiment complemented her belief in contingency. Life may be precarious, but nothing is foreclosed; something may go awry, but then it may go aright. In such a world hope remains as realistic as despondency.

Balthasar, on the other hand, was a man who could find the clouds around every silver lining. Still, despite his temperamental hedging, hopelessness was as foreign to him as it was to Magdalena. Consider, for example, his effort to console himself when news came from brother Paul that Balthasar's new gray colt, the younger of two he had recently bought and an animal he dearly loved, had been stricken with a serious illness which, according to Paul, would bring an end to any joy Balthasar might have found in the creature. "If, as still may happen, he overcomes his illness, it may strengthen his resistance and prove useful to him," Balthasar reasoned. "Should he die, he is still dearer to me than a man, and I must consider all the money I have lost." Balthasar hoped for the best when faced with the worst, and he overcame adversity by treating it as something routine.

Self-reliance bounded by the will of God—these were the terms in which Magdalena and Balthasar understood their lives. Such self-understanding both emboldened and limited them, a source of consolation or inspiration, humility or resolve, as the circumstances warranted. It fit a world like theirs that was between absolutes, still believing in the power of God while discovering the powers of man.

# VII

# ℱAMILIES PAST AND PRESENT

If there is a mistake worse than believing that the present and the past are the same, it is thinking they are completely different. There may be worlds of difference between yesterday and today, but the past is not a different world. We are continuous. The past draws us to itself and we learn from it precisely because we discover ourselves there under altered conditions.

Today historians of the family stress discontinuity with the past, viewing the transition from the traditional to the modern family as a virtual revolution in structure and sentiment. The pre-modern family, we are told, had been strictly patriarchal, a hierarchically structured workplace whose authoritarian nature depersonalized family relationships. High mortality and frequent remarriage also placed obstacles in the way of deep and enduring personal relationships among family members; there was neither sufficient time together nor stability enough for intimacy to develop within most families. In the world of the past, women were the underclass, nowhere worse off than in marriage, where they became involuntary broom-sweeps and bearers of children. The credulity of an age easily obsessed with sin and the Devil added to the joylessness of family life by justifying coercion and even cruelty within it. According to modern historians, the emotional and moral life of the family brightened only when the home ceased to be the family workshop, medicine increased life spans, and science diminished superstition. Then the cold, impersonal, authoritarian traditional family could be transformed into the warm, private, egalitarian modern family. To borrow from the title of a recent book on the subject, the transition from pre-industrial to modern times has been a transition "from patriarchy to partnership."

The world of Magdalena and Balthasar is not one that modern historians have prepared us to find. In structure and organization, their home closely approximated traditional family life. Although Balthasar did not manufacture on the premises, and for a period of sixteen years was away at least two months each year and on four occasions for as long as six, their home remained the site of his business, a warehouse into which goods were received and out of which they were disbursed. The family and business economies occupied a great part of their day. Having a business in the home, however, seems actually to have helped rather than hindered the relationship; it was when business took Balthasar away from home for extended periods that suspicion and argument seem most seriously to have threatened the marriage.

Like the vast majority of pre-modern people, neither Magdalena nor Balthasar had a wide range of vocational options, yet both accepted their lots in life as meaningful, self-fulfilling work. Over the years, Balthasar came to despise his work, and he managed to escape briefly into the more tranquil life of a country gentleman a few years before his death. Magdalena on occasion resented Balthasar's business for taking him away from her, but never for a moment did she wish to trade places with him. She recognized his business as burdensome and debilitating, preparing him for an early grave (she outlived her husband, who was only five years her senior, by forty-two years). When Magdalena contemplated his work, she did not envy the man in her life nor did she think him to be specially advantaged. Whereas Balthasar admired the variety and gaiety in her life, she pitied him as one stuck in a vocational rut, mere chattel to his firm.

Theirs was also a patriarchal family: all household members—Magdalena, the servants, and little Balthasar —readily acknowledged Balthasar's "rule." But Magdalena's submission to her husband's authority was nowhere more abject than on those occasions when she gave him instructions on what he should be doing on her behalf; and the same might be said of little Balthasar. Balthasar wore his patriarchal status solemnly, but he exercised it lightly. Being paterfamilias inhibited neither his admiration for Magdalena's domestic skills nor his outspoken praise of her professional competence when she expertly managed their business affairs in Nuremberg. The two routinely shared authority, and Balthasar readily sought and deferred to Magdalena's business judgment.

The quality of their marriage and family life was arguably not very different from what we today deem "modern." They remained in their fashion emotionally involved with each other over the years. Magdalena seems always to have had a bride's enthusiasm for her husband, and Balthasar was still "wishing" her melons in season from Lucca after thirteen years of marriage. No more than their work did the constant reminders of mortality all around them bar intimacy or dilute affection. Indeed, the more benumbed they were by personal tragedy or exhausted by business hardship, the more readily and eloquently did they pour their hearts out to each other.

As a parent, Balthasar self-consciously cultivated his

role as disciplinarian. Yet little Balthasar's requests were more often than not filled, and the child was indulged by both parents. Perhaps if they had had many children or had been impoverished it might have changed their relationship to each other and to their children. Their conjugal and parental feelings, however, give every evidence of running deep and being resilient. In a correspondence that records sixteen years of private and public calamity, they never mention the Devil or witches. Magdalena and Balthasar believe in God and purgative medicine. From a modern point of view, these were primitive aids, not always worthy of their devotion. Contemporary medical science certainly did Balthasar at least as much harm as good, and God appears not to have done as much for either as contemporary theology might reasonably have led them to believe he might. Yet the pair's devotion to medicine and religion persisted, becoming more experimental and detailed in the medical sphere, simpler and more circumscribed in the religious. Physicians intrigued them more than did God, but they found God, in the end, to be the more necessary and trustworthy. Such credulity was of course circumstantial, bound up with their culture and utilitarian. But they also reflected privately and independently on their experience. Theirs was a philosophy of life that can also be called their own. They speak for themselves as well as for an age.

# EPILOGUE

Our story, unfortunately, is blurred at the end as it was at the beginning. The sources do not exist to give it a definite resolution. Balthasar, we know, died on July 13, 1600. Since late 1596, the management of a small estate, Holenstein, in the Upper Palatinate, not far from Nuremberg, competed with his diminishing mercantile business for his time and attention. In the last of Magdalena's letters to him at the Frankfurt fair, written on March 22, 1597, she hopes that God will help him depart Frankfurt soon and stay well and that they may "soon be together in Holenstein." They were now going back and forth between two homes.

When, on December 11, 1598, Balthasar writes the last of his extant letters to Magdalena in Nuremberg, he is in Neuburg on the Danube, engaged both as a merchant and as a new landowner. He is at a district diet and in very good company, surrounded by the political elite of the region and feeling a little out of place. As always, he finds himself besieged. He has plans to go directly to Holenstein upon the diet's conclusion. However, he expects an eight- to nine-day delay because of the proceedings, a part of which directly concerns him. He claims to have been slandered and embarrassed before the diet by one Sebastian Saurzapff, a man he describes as a recognized "scoundrel." Apparently there is litigation brewing involving Holenstein. Balthasar has appealed to the Count Palatine of Sulzbach, Otto Heinrich, for support and he is addressing the diet in writing on the matter. He is confident of vindication and stiff punishment for Saurzapff, and he is making friends and allies in high places. He tells Magdalena in a postscript that he will be traveling back with the sheriff and the clerk of their district and that they will be spending the night with them: "Therefore you may in your free moments want to get a little something prepared in the kitchen."

Balthasar died nineteen months later. Magdalena not only outlived him, she outlived all their siblings as well. She died on February 14, 1642, at the rare old age of eighty-seven.

What became of her during these years without Balthasar and the siblings and in-laws who had been so large a part of her life? The family genealogy indicates that she did not remarry. We can imagine her going back and forth between Nuremberg and Holenstein, spending time with both old and new family members and friends. The one person from our story who had been a vital part of her life and who lived as long as she was little Madela (d. 1652). Madela married Johann Jakob Löffelholz of Kolberg in 1619, and they were together for twelve years before his death. Perhaps there were children from the marriage. Perhaps they, like their mother, were cared for and enriched by their great-aunt and gave her some happiness in return. Until the discovery of new sources tells us otherwise, one would like to think that Magdalena's life remained as full as it was long.

# NOTES

### INTRODUCTION

**12**
in intellectual history.: *Briefwechsel Balthasar Paumgartners des Jüngeren mit seiner Gattin Magdalena, geb. Behaim (1582–1598)*, ed. Georg Steinhausen (Tübingen, 1895), pp. v–vi.

**13**
to the point.: Carl Koch, "Die Sprache der Magdalena und des Balthasar Paumgartner in ihrem Briefwechsel. Zur Geschichte der Nürnberger Mundart und zur nhd. Schriftsprache im 16. Jahrhundert," *Mitteilungen aus dem Germanischen Nationalmuseum* (Nuremberg, 1909), pp. 152–54. Beyond Koch's study of their language, the only other attempts to deal with the letters that I am aware of is Hans Bösch's prospectus, "Balthasar Paumgartner d. J. von Nürnberg, ein Besucher der Frankfurter Messe 1583–1597," *Bamberger Stadt- und Land-Kalender auf das Jahr 1900* (Bamberg, 1900), pp. 3–7, and Georg Steinhausen's occasional references in his survey of early modern German mercantile history, *Der Kaufmann in der deutschen Vergangenheit* (Leipzig, 1899), esp. pp. 89–98.

### I: A CITY OF MERCHANTS

**15**
" '. . . Deceaves every land.' ": William Smith, "A Description of the Cittie of Noremberg . . . 1594, übersetzt," introduced by Karlheinz Goldmann, translated by William Roach,

*Mitteilungen des Vereins für Geschichte der Stadt Nürnberg (MVGN)* 48 (1958): 206.

15
Nuremberg's success: Contemporary maps of the city, *ibid.*, 206–9; their evolution is discussed by Karl Schaefer, "Des H. Braun Prospekt der Stadt Nürnberg vom Jahre 1608 und seine Vorläufer," *MVGN* 12 (1896): 3–84.

17
crafts and trades: Rudolf Endres, "Zur Einwohnerzahl und Bevölkerungsstruktur Nürnberg im 15./16. Jahrhundert," *MVGN* 57 (1970): 246–48, 256–57.

18
". . . and obedience.": Smith, "Description," 216.

18
the Small Council: *Ibid.*, 216–18; Gerald Strauss, *Nuremberg in the Sixteenth Century* (New York, 1966), pp. 61–62.

19
at least twice that.: Gustav Aubin, "Bartholomäus Viatis. Ein Nürnberger Grosskaufmann vor dem Dreissigjährigen Kriege," *Vierteljahrschrift für Sozial- und Wirtschaftsgeschichte (VSWG)* 33 (1940): 156; Endres, "Einwohnerzahl," 256–58, 259.

19
basic material assistance.: Endres, "Einwohnerzahl," 256–57, 261–62, 268.

20
3,000 to Viatis.: Aubin, "Viatis," 154; Endres, "Einwohnerzahl," 263; *Briefwechsel*, April 5, 1593, p. 182; Apr. 8, 1593, p. 185. *Cf.* also Gerhard Seibold, "Die Imhoffsche Handelsgesellschaft in den Jahren 1579–1635," *MVGN* 64 (1977): 210–14.

20
". . . to have it again.": Endres, "Einwohnerzahl," 259; Strauss, *Nuremberg*, p. 8; Smith, "Description," 214–16.

20
half a year old.: Smith, "Description," 222.

22
whipping and banishment.: *Ibid.*, 233.

22
Augsburg in particular.: Strauss, *Nuremberg*, pp. 145–49; Johannes Müller, "Die Finanzpolitik des Nürnberger Rates in der zweiten Hälfte des 16. Jahrhunderts," *VSWG* 7 (1909): 1–63.

22
a generation to replenish.: Endres, "Einwohnerzahl," 250.

23
age of Dürer.: Jeffrey Chipps Smith, *Nuremberg: A Renaissance City, 1500–1618* (Austin, 1983).

23

The Behaims and the Paumgartners: For the reconstruction of basic family relationships I have drawn primarily on genealogical charts. For the Behaims, Johann Gottfried Biedermann, *Geschlechtsregister des hochadelichen Patriciats zu Nürnberg* (Bayreuth, 1748), Tables VII, VIII, IX; for the Paumgartners, the Nuremberg Stadtarchiv's reconstruction of the "Stammbaum der Nürnberger Familie Paumgartner," *Wappen und Geschlechtsbücher*, nr. 46 (7); and for the Scheurls, Biedermann, *Geschlechtsregister*, Tables 441–442.

For the Paumgartners, one may also consult Georg Andreas Will, *Nürnbergisches Gelehrter-Lexicon*, III, VII (Nürnberg/ Altdorf, 1757, 1806), and Wilhelm Krag, *Die Paumgartner von Nürnberg und Augsburg: Ein Beitrag zur Handelsgeschichte des 15. und 16. Jahrhunderts* (Munich/Leipzig, 1919). Much of this material, however, is dated and focused on the Paumgartners of Augsburg rather than on those of Nuremberg, with precious little on Nuremberg family fortunes in the second half of the century. More helpful general treatments of Nuremberg merchants are Georg Steinhausen, *Der Kaufmann in der deutschen Vergangenheit;* Gustav Bub, *Alte Nürnberger Familien: Beiträge zur Kulturgeschichte der Stadt Nürnberg*, I (Hersbruck, 1930); Ludwig Veit, *Handel und Wandel mit aller Welt: Aus Nürnbergs grosser Zeit* (Munich, 1960); and Gerhard Pfeiffer, ed., *Nürnberg: Geschichte einer europäischen Stadt* (Munich, 1971), chs. 30–32, 50.

25

reads the entry.: This information was kindly supplied me by Dr. Frhr. von Brandenstein, Archivrat, Landeskirchliche Archiv, Nuremberg. On Balthasar's birth and death dates, see also Steinhausen, *Briefwechsel*, p. vii; Koch, "Die Sprache," p. 152.

## II: Lovers

27

". . . heart's dearest treasure.": *Briefwechsel Balthasar Paumgartners des Jüngeren mit seiner Gattin Magdalena, geb. Behaim (1582–1598)*, ed. Georg Steinhausen (Tübingen, 1895), Oct. 24, 1582, p. 3; Dec. 25, 1582, p. 13; Jan. 1, 1583, p. 19. All dates below are from this source unless otherwise noted. I have checked Steinhausen's transcriptions against a microfilm copy of the manuscript letters and found them to be faithful to the originals, accurate in details, and without deletions. About twenty of the one hundred and sixty-nine letters are now faded to the point of being barely legible.

27

". . . friendly and sincere greetings.": Oct. 24, 1582, p. 5; Dec. 25, 1582, p. 17.

27

". . . rather than write them.": "Wöllest mitt meiner böesen geschryfft (die du kaum wirst lesen können) inn eil also für lieb nehmen. Gib einen bösen unwilligen schreiber; woltt dir diesenn viel lieber selber fürlesen, dann schreibenn." Dec. 22, 1582, pp. 12–13.

27

". . . garden of joy.": "Freüdengärttlin"—a favored term in the betrothal letters that fades after the marriage. Oct. 24, 1582, p. 5; Dec. 15, 1582, pp. 6, 10.

28

"bleeding-day gift": "Die beste aderlas-schenck." Dec. 25, 1582, p. 13; Aug. 27, 1584, p. 64.

28

manger of Christ.: Dec. 15, 1582, p. 10; Dec. 25, 1582, pp. 16–17. This was a common custom.

28

". . . and Sanctifier.": Dec. 22, 1582, p. 11; see also Jan. 1, 1592, p. 154.

28

who first transcribed them.: Georg Steinhausen, *Geschichte des deutschen Briefes*, II (Berlin, 1889), pp. 181–82, 189. Steinhausen calls attention, however, to genuine spontaneity in the letters of non–formally educated women, among whom one may surely count Magdalena.

32

first night in Lucca.: "Ich hab mir das schayden den letzten abendt, ich von dir ginng, ja nichtt so schwer fürgesetztt, alls es mir hernacher gedeyett hatt. Dastu mir inn deinem obern stüblin also unntter den armen hinwegk sunckest, hab ich mir nymmermehr auss dem syn schlagen müegenn, unnd sind seider ja wennig, wennig stund hingangen, inn welchen ich nicht an dich gedacht hett. . . . Vergangne freyttags alls die ehrste nachtt ich allhie inn unnserm [haus] geschlaffenn, hatt mir stettigs von dir geträumett; verhoff nichtts dann alles guetss bedeutten soll." *Briefwechsel*, Oct. 24, 1582, p. 4.

33

as promptly as he might have.: Dec. 15, 1582, p. 6.

33

lost business opportunities.: Oct. 24, 1582, p. 4.

33

"So let this anger . . ."; Dec. 15, 1582, p. 7.

33
"all kinds of strange thoughts": "Du meldest unnttr anderm inn deinem brieff, ich soll dich mitt schreibenn nichtt mehr so lang [warten] lassenn: wer wyss, ob ich dich bey den böesen bey euch regirenden leüfften mehr finnde! Mitt solchem hastu mir nichtt wennig ahnfechtonng unnd allerlay seltzame gedanncken gemachtt." *Ibid.*, p. 10.

36
as mutual anger!: "Und das du mir schreibst, wir woln den zorn zugleich mit ein ander auflasen gon, weis ich von keinem nit: nims aug anderst nit, als scherzweis auf. Got las uns aug nimer mer kein augenblick solgen versugen unser leben lang." Dec. 25, 1582, p. 14.

36
illness and disease.: See page 118 and note.

36
"completely bad . . . writing": "Gar besen krumen schreiben und kindichsen." Dec. 25, 1582, p. 17.

36
Frau Flexner was widowed.: *Ibid.*, pp. 15–16.

37
"emptyhanded" before a mailbox.: Jan. 22, 1583, p. 23.

37
as the bishop's guest.: Feb. 9, 1583, pp. 26–27.

37
"Don't overdo it . . .": "Bitt ich dich . . . bey einem gleichen bleiben zu lassen und so köstlichen nicht zu machen." Jan. 19, 1583, p. 21.

38
". . . dearest treasure.": Jan. 1, 1583, p. 19.

38
"With patience . . .": "Mitt geduld komptt man weytt unnd übrwynndet viel." Dec. 22, 1582, p. 12.

38
likely to be there.: *Ibid.;* Dec. 25, 1582, pp. 12–14.

39
". . . I would be embarrassed.": "Herzlieber schaz, es zabelt iezund in lenger in mer. Weis nit, ist des farns schult gen Altorff oder was es ist, das sich so unniz macht in mir. Denck aber, Got und die zeit wer uns solgs wol sehen lasen. Erschrick oft recht, wan es sich so reckt. Herzeter scaz, las den prief nitt lichen vor iemundt: schem mich sunst!" July 1, 1584, p. 49. Regarding Magdalena's pregnancy, she reports in her letter of July 24 that she is making a baby's pillow. *Briefwechsel*, pp. 151, 158.

43
". . . our lives to share.": "Wan der mittwog kumpt, so

frei ich mich, dir zu schreiben, und denck, nun haben wir aber acht tag weniger zusamen." Dec. 30, 1591, p. 151.

43
". . . my life long.": Nov. 17, 1591, p. 134; Jan. 6, 1592, p. 154; April 1590, p. 105.

43-44
efficient maid.: N.d., 1590, p. 139; April 1593, p. 183; Dec. 30, 1591, p. 152.

44
tempted to rush.: Nov. 25, 1591, p. 137.

44
salted crackling.: Aug. 27, 1584, p. 64.

44
". . . fast so long.": Sept. 2, 1589, p. 99.

44
for two fairs.: Sept. 14, 1589, p. 101.

45
". . . some up to you.": "Dir solche hinnauswünschen." July 18, 1584, pp. 53, 56; Aug. 14, 1584, p. 63; Aug. 10, 1594, p. 236; Aug. 17, 1594, p. 239.

45
health has returned.: "Allerlay unnd schier böese nachgedannckenn." June 29, 1594, p. 214.

45
more than two weeks.: "Wol sorg hab, offt geschehen wer, so du meine brieff zulezt sparst, dir der zeit zurinen wer zu zeiden. Bit aber, herzeter schaz, wolst mich uber 8 oder 14 tag zum alerlengsten nit lasen, ehr desto kierzer abpregen welst." Dec. 1, 1591, p. 139.

46
". . . so much to do.": Dec. 9, 1591, p. 141.

46
". . . This for now!": "So vil ir [in?] die wogen an des Pfinzings hachzeit mit mir gedanzt haben, haben dein im besten gedacht und gefragt, wan schreiben von dir gehabt. So` hab ich aber gedeuchst und gesagt, vor acht tagen, wan schön 3 wogen! Nun auf dis mal nit mer!" Ibid., p. 143.

46
return from Lucca.: Dec. 23, 1591, p. 143.

46
". . . except you!": "Alein an dir gemangelt." Ibid., p. 144.

46
". . . you are excused.": "Mit sunderlichen herzensfreuten hab ich vergangen samstag deinen prief empfangen, auf welgen ich mein regnung vor 3 wogen gemachet hab, das ich vermeinet, schreiben auf mein erstes zu bekumen. Aber wol denck, du ein wenig mer den alein mir zu schreiben habst,

derhalben endtschultigett bist." December 1591, pp. 148–149.

47
pages long.: Dec. 25, 1591, p. 145.

47
". . . business correspondence.": Jan. 8, 1592, p. 157.

47
". . . once and for all!": *Ibid.*

48
"completely annoyed" with him: "Es mir gar and thut, das du mir so selten schreibst da mir die weil 3mal lenger ist, den vorhin leider." April 1593, p. 83.

48
arrival of her letters: Aug. 1, 1594, p. 229.

48
". . . mail priority." June 1, 1594, p. 204.

51
try another place?: April 4, 1594, p. 218; Aug. 1, 1594, p. 226.

51
". . . lies ahead.": "Mein herzeter schaz, wie wirtt mir nor sein, wan dich wider sich und hab. Es dunckt mich ieh lang sein nunmer. Got helf uns die 2 monet von iezt on aug uberwinden!" Aug. 8, 1594, pp. 234–35.

51
depart Lucca.: Aug. 17, 1594.

52
". . . dear Paumgartner.": Aug. 29, 1594, p. 240.

53
". . . half a day there.": Aug. 29, 1594, pp. 243–44.

53
it will occasion.: Sept. 28, 1594, pp. 255–56.

53
than does Balthasar.: Sept. 14, 1594, p. 252; Sept. 18, 1594, p. 253; Sept. 28, 1594, p. 255.

55
a housekeeping drudge.: "Bitt dich drum, wen du zu Meinz oder im badt etwas selzsams sihest, wolst mir was mittpringen. Vergist dus, den hab ich genug an dir, davir ich Gott zu dancken hab. . . . Und weis dir sunst, herzlieber Paumgartner, nichts, dan das du deiner wol warnemst; nit weis, wie du in der kugen drin versehen wirst sein. Mecht ie wol bey dir sein. Ist lang auf meiner wal gestanden, ob wir, ich und schbager Paulus, nit die 3 schimel on ein ring kizla spanen und farn mit hinab. Gedacht, doch nein, hast mirs nit erlaubt, so ging unkosten aug drauf; und dieweil du gesagt, derfst mein nit vir dis mal, hab ichs eingestelt.

Sunst hab ich die wogen zu sudeln und aufzufegen zu lasen." April 19, 1596, pp. 263–64.


III: PARTNERS

56
sources and markets.: Ernst Walter Zeeden, *Deutsche Kultur in der frühen Neuzeit* (Frankfurt am Main, 1968), pp. 116–22; Aubin, "Viatis," 145–57; W. Schultheiss, "Der Nürnberger Grosskaufmann und Diplomat Andreas I Imhoff und seine Zeit (1491–1579)," *Mitteilungen aus der Stadtbibliothek Nürnberg* 6 (1957).

59
"completely useless.": *Briefwechsel,* May 7, 1572, pp. 2–3.

60
an "eloquent and skillful" woman: Dec. 15, 1582, pp. 9–10; Dec. 25, 1582, p. 14.

60
". . . a day passes.": "Hab ye schlechtte freüde: da man doben im bad, auch alhie übral frölich ist, bin ich stil unnd traurig, ja mag offt gar nichtts redenn. Mir schier selber feind, also meucken mag. Viel leütt, die mich zuvor gekand, offt darumb beschreyen, wiewol mein lebentag nye gern viel wortt gemachtt hab. Mein gröeste freüd, so ich allhie hab, ist den sonntag abend, wann die brief kommen, deren ich allwegenn mit grossem verlangen verwartte. Nuhn, es gehett Gott lob all tag ein tag hinwegk." July 18, 1584, p. 55.

61
complete ruin there.: "Wann mir nun der lieb Gott bald widerumb aus diesem Franckforttischem fegfeür zu dir heimb nach haus verhülffe, wan ich ditz Franckfortts abermals schon so gnueg, alls wann mit löfeln darvon geessen hett. Hab sorg, werde es einsmals von freyen stucken verreden, nymmermehr herabzukommen. Dann besorg, heütt oder morgen ainest mein grab gar sein möcht." March 26, 1586, p. 78.

61
". . . as I have planned it.":"Gehett mir allso garnichtt nach meinem sinn, mich allso schier darein ergebenn muess, das mir nymmer nichtts nach meinem willenn, alls vor mir hab, forttgehett." Sept. 19, 1591, p. 123.

61
"here from everywhere.": March 20, 1591, pp. 108–9.

61
to all travelers.: Sept. 2, 1591, p. 117; Dec. 25,1591, p. 147.

61
never assured.: July 27, 1594, p. 226.

63
out of handkerchiefs.: Dec. 25, 1591, p. 147; April 13, 1595,
p. 258.

63
". . . common folk.": Dec. 25, 1591, pp. 147–48; Aug. 3,
1594, p. 232.

63
to pursue them.: "Umb das geltt sehr haiss unnd saur von
den leütten heraussgehett." Sept. 17, 1584, p. 68.

63
". . . to be at home.": "Bin nunmehr inn der grösten mühe
und arbaytt, wolltt meins thails, es were schon unnd wol
verrichtt, darumb gern ettwas gutts schuldig sein woltt. Nun,
ich muss mich nun mitt gewaltt herdurch fretten, wird noch
manchmal schreyen unnd zanckens gnug geben, darfür wol
viel lieber daheimb sein woltt." March 28, 1585, p. 73.

63
and subordinates.: March 10, 1592, p. 168.

63
cousin Paul Scheurl.: Sept. 13, 1592, p. 176.

63
". . . and also cursing.": April 5, 1593, p. 181.

64
". . . cannot always have.": "Aber wie mans gern hett,
wird mans doch nichtt allzeitt haben khönnen." April 15,
1593, p. 186.

64
". . . have been heard.": Balthasar clearly includes himself
among the "verstendige und geschicktte khauffleütt" who
could and should have been consulted. Sept. 12, 1596, p. 272;
Sept. 18, 1596, p. 274.

64
". . . with a spoon.": March 19, 1597, p. 279. See also
above, page 60 (1586).

64
should Caspar succeed: March 22, 1583, p. 31.

66
". . . must contend!": July 18, 1584, pp. 54–55.

66
Magdalena scoffs.: July 22, 1584, p. 58.

66
Magdalena wishes.: September 1584, p. 68.

66
". . . accompanied him!": Jan. 20, 1592, p. 161; on Balthasar's run-in with him, letter of Sept. 17, 1588, p. 92.

67
". . . put into jail.": Nov. 17, 1591, pp. 135–36; Dec. 25,
1591, p. 146.

68
than Balthasar.: Aug. 8, 1594, pp. 233–34; Aug. 15, 1594,
pp. 237–38; Aug. 29, 1594, p. 241; Sept. 18, 1594, p. 254;
Sept. 6, 1594, p. 248.

68
". . . its own masters.": July 17, 1596, p. 267.

69
currency rates.: Sept. 18, 1596, p. 274.

69
". . . my regimen here.": "Mir ist lieb das daussen so viel
guetts muhtts, gasterey, hochzeitten unnd schier gar des
schlarauffenland ist, unnd aber noch lieber, das ich selb nitt
darbey sein darff, allso manchs übrigen schäedlichen truncks
dardurch überhebtt bin. Bin, glaub mir, bey meinem ordinary
allhie viel gesunndter." Jan. 1, 1592, p. 153.

70
". . . the immoderate drinking.": Jan. 8, 1592, p. 158; Smith,
"Description," p. 228; Briefwechsel, Jan. 20, 1592, p. 160.
See also April 5, 1593, p. 181, where Balthasar assures Magdalena that the cold weather will not become an occasion for
him to "drink too much."

71
Footnote: Smith, "Description," p. 226.

72
maintained the receipts.: Dec. 15, 1582, p. 9; March 14,
1583, p. 28; March 22, 1583, pp. 30–31.

72
regular items.: Sept. 9, 1591, pp. 120–21; Aug. 29, 1594,
p. 244; June 1, 1594, p. 203; Aug. 1, 1594, pp. 227–28; Mar.
3, 1593, pp. 178–79; July 10, 1594, p. 219.

72
still cold.: Sept. 14, 1589, p. 102; Sept. 21, 1589, pp. 102–03;
April 1, 1587, pp. 80–81; March 18, 1597, p. 276.

73
Cambrai flax.: April 12, 1596, p. 261.

73
". . . they never will.": Dec. 25, 1591, p. 146; Jan. 15, 1592,
p. 159.

73
her brother's wedding.: April 18, 1594, p. 193.

74
magnitude of her tasks.: March 4, 1594, p. 191.

74
line of duty.: April 1593, p. 184.

74
and glaziers.: Sept. 7, 1587, p. 84; Sept. 9, 1589, p. 100–101.

74
Balthasar's return.: N.d. 1587, pp. 81–82.

74
". . . stroke the fox's tail": "Wirst dich also zu verhaltten unnd ihr den fuchsschwantz wol zu streichen wissenn, daran gar nichtt zweyfle." Dec. 15, 1582, p. 7.

75
"in your place.": "Bis morgen zu nacht also donerstag sol ich aug schmorozen mit der Carl Pfinzingin, hat die heimladung, mus mich halt an dein stad einsteln." Nov. 17, 1591, p. 136; Dec. 1, 1591, p. 140.

75
(Lebkuchen).: Sept. 13, 1592, p. 174.

75
on Balthasar's behalf.: Sept. 6, 1592, p. 172.

75
a gift for his son.: June 20, 1594, p. 207; April 23, 1596, p. 266.

75
maintained the accounts.: May 6, 1594, p. 197; July 13, 1594, p. 221.

75
Khürn's death.: April 1, 1587, pp. 80–81.

75–76
best price it can fetch.: June 13, 1584, p. 45.

76
". . . also pleases me.": Ibid., Sept. 9, 1592, p. 173; Sept. 13, 1592, p. 175.

76
would have been prevented.: "Wan du mir halt nor von erst die farb hest geschriben, het ich dirs wider hinein geschriben, das es nit diglich wer. Nun, es ist geschehen." Aug. 27, 1584, p. 65.

77
"so diplomatically.": "Mit glimpf." Sept. 9, 1585, p. 75; Sept. 14, 1585, p. 76.

77
wish him good luck.: Nov. 11, 1591, p. 133; Nov. 17, 1591, p. 135.

77
"no man in the house.": April 24, 1594, p. 194.

77
rather expected it.: May 2, 1594, p. 196; July 1, 1594, p. 203.

78
from Jakob Imhoff.: July 7, 1584, p. 48; Aug. 15, 1594, p. 238; Aug. 8, 1594.

78
Christian of Anhalt.: Sept. 5, 1592, p. 171.

78
next founder's day.: July 1, 1584, p. 48.

78
". . . Polish manner.": "Haben wir gehabt vil richt und wenig zu esen, so gozjemerlich gekocht gewesen auf ir polnichse weis." July 7, 1584, p. 50.

81
"a ham or three.": September 1583, p. 37 (sugar); Sept. 2, 1591, p. 117; Sept. 13, 1592, p. 174; April 1593, p. 148; April 10, 1584, pp. 39–40 (cheeses); Sept. 2, 1591, p. 117; Sept. 6, 1592, p. 172; April 1593, p. 184; Sept. 17, 1588, p. 93 (quinces); Sept. 2, 1589, p. 99; Sept. 9, 1589, p. 101; Sept. 13, 1592, p. 174; Sept. 17, 1588, p. 93 (Zellernuts); Sept. 9, 1589, p. 101 and passim; Sept. 2, 1589, p. 99 (pears); Sept. 9, 1589, p. 101; Sept. 13, 1592, p. 174; Dec. 23, 1591, p. 44 (fennel); Jan. 6, 1592, p. 156 (olive oil); Jan. 13, 1592, p. 164 (green nuts); March 12, 1592, p. 167 (ham); April 1593, p. 184.

81
velvet, and damask.: Aug. 27, 1584, p. 65; Sept. 2, 1591, p. 117; Sept. 10, 1588, p. 91; Sept. 17, 1588, p. 93; Dec. 9, 1591, p. 142; Apr. 2, 1593, p. 180; June 24, 1594, p. 211; Aug. 29, 1594, p. 242.

81
thread.: April 10, 1584, pp. 39–40; Sept. 18, 1594, p. 254; Jan. 6, 1592, p. 155; Jan. 13, 1592, p. 164.

81
damask one.: Oct. 20, 1591, p. 124.

81
". . . thick, lustrous.: "Schön grob und glanzig." Dec. 30, 1591, p. 151.

81
". . . in every letter": "Welst mir nitt vir ubel haben, das ich dir in meinem schreiben imer etwas abbedele." Dec. 9, 1591, p. 142.

81
precise information.: Jan. 8, 1592, p. 158; Jan. 29, 1592, p. 162.

82
". . . with a dress.": June 24, 1584, p. 211. See Steinhau-

sen's reasons for dating the letter in 1584 rather than 1594, as the museum's archivists had originally done. *Ibid.* Steinhausen does not connect this particular passage with Magdalena's pregnancy, which is even more striking evidence of the letter's misdating.

82
thirty-three Italian crowns.: Aug. 29, 1594, pp. 243–44.

82
over the fly.: Kent R. Greenfield, *Sumptuary Law in Nürnberg: A Study in Paternal Government* (Baltimore, 1918), p. 115.

83
addition to his wardrobe.: "Nichtt auss hochfahrtt, sondern grosser hoher nottdurfft einen neühen wolfspeltz haben muess." June 29, 1594, p. 215; Aug. 1, 1594, p. 227.

85
a very proper spacing.: August Jegel, "Altnürnberger Hochzeitsbrauch und Eherecht, bes. bis zum Ausgang des 16. Jahrhunderts," *MVGN* 44 (1953): 264; Steven Ozment, *When Fathers Ruled: Family Life in Reformation Europe* (Cambridge, Mass., 1983), p. 38.

85
"no more old men.": "Einen schönen jungenn, ihr angenehmen gesellen, wöllen keinen altten mehr." Jan. 22, 1583, p. 24.

85
nor Magdalena.: December 1591, p. 150.

86
twenty-sixth child.: Feb. 9, 1583, p. 27; March 13, 1597, p. 276.

86
view of the marriage.: "So ein schön menchss ist." Jan. 20, 1592, p. 161.

86
"too easy remarriages.": Endres, "Einwohnerzahl," p. 263.

86
love and loyalty.: "Vergis halt mein einmal nit so balt!" July 22, 1584, p. 58.

87
Smith disapproved.: Smith, "Description," pp. 225–26.

87
marriage plans.: Jan. 21, 1585, pp. 70–71.

88
her wedding night.: Aug. 1, 1594, p. 230.

88
father of her child.: *Ibid.*, p. 228.

88
". . . extremely well.": Sept. 6, 1592, p. 172.


IV: PARENTS

90
". . . are still in good health.": Jan. 21, 1585, p. 70.
92
". . . to write to you.": March 29, 1588, p. 90.
92
". . . bringing him one.": Sept. 9, 1589, p. 101.
92
". . . and a purse.": N.d., probably early 1590, p. 108.
92
". . . may bring him.": March 22, 1591, p. 112.
92-93
". . . like about this.": Sept. 2, 1591, p. 117.
93
some new clothes.: Dec. 9, 1591, p. 141.
93
"requests" of them.: "Befehlen," "ermahnen." Steinhausen
calls attention to this custom in the relationship between husband and wife. Geschichte des deutschen Briefes, p. 168. But
Magdalena also reports her son's requests as commands or
admonishments.
93
". . . doing him harm.": "Er is beslich uber das lernen zu
pringen, der stal thut im vil zu leid." N.d., early 1590, p. 108.
93
". . . greet him warmly.": Nov. 11, 1591, p. 133.
93
writing at night.: Dec. 23, 1591, p. 144.
94
between them.: March 30, 1589, p. 97.
94
". . . better than he.": Sept. 21, 1589, p. 103.
94
". . . not, I will bring him nothing.": Sept. 6, 1591, p. 120.
94
". . . with the schoolmaster.": June 5, 1591, p. 114.
94
billing a client.: "Mitt einander abrechnenn." Sept. 5, 1591,
p. 119.
94
". . . and I will bring him nothing.": "Sonst nichtt eins
bleiben." Nov. 9, 1591, p. 131.

95
on the subject.: Nov. 17, 1591, p. 136.

95
". . . your loving son].": "Lieber vater, ich bit dich, du welest mir ein welsche cruna zum neien yar rausschicken, ich wil gar frum sein und Got fleisig vir dich biten. Balthasla Paumgartner d.l.s." Dec. 30, 1591, p. 152 (sent in fact with Magdalena's letter of Nov. 17).

95
". . . gift personally.": Jan. 1, 1592, p. 154.

95
". . . in my letters.": Jan. 6, 1592, p. 155.

96
". . . as you please.": Dec. 9, 1591, p. 141; December 1591, p. 149.

96
". . . studies diligently.": Jan. 15, 1592, p. 160.

96
colds and coughing.: Mar. 24, 1585, p. 72; n.d., 1585, p. 79.

96
apply the medicine.: March 23, 1588, p. 85.

97
such treatment.: March 29, 1588, p. 90.

97
in Nuremberg.: April 1, 1589, p. 99.

97
". . . during your absence.": April 7, 1590, p. 104.

97
the high fever.: April 1590, p. 105.

97
with measles.: Dec. 30, 1591, p. 151.

98
". . . know joy again.": Feb. 17, 1592, p. 166.

98
". . . his divine will.": March 12, 1592, p. 167.

100
". . . do better soon.": "Lieber vadter. Ich hörs gern, das du gesundt bist na kumen und bitt dich, du wolst mir ein kleins pferla mittbringen. Freg nur den Meringer, wu mas kaufft, mitt kalbshautt uberzugen, und 2 bar stimpf, ein leibsfarbs und ein schwartz bar. Ich will gar frum sein und flucks lernen und nim mitt dem schreibn vergutt; ich wils bald busser lernen. Dattum in eill." March 1591, pp. 110–11. Little Balthasar goes on to ask his father in a postscript to tell servant Hans also to bring him and Hans's daughter, Anala, little Balthasar's playmate, something.

100
". . . buy him one.": Sept. 9, 1591, p. 121.

100
". . . bring me a real horse.": Dec. 23, 1591, p. 144; March 12, 1592, p. 167.

101
". . . come to him!": March 15, 1592, pp. 168–69.

101
". . . tolled for him.": "Mus also gedencken, so balt in gehabt, nit unser gewesen ist und leider ein vergebliche freutt gehabtt haben. Mus mich demnach nor mit Got zufriden geben, dan ich leider sich, nit mer davon pring, dan schbegung, bösen kofp und böse augen. Mus mirs ausschlagen, so vil mir nor miglich. Desgleichen wolst du aug thon, herzliebster schaz, und dirs aus dem sin schlagen und gedultig sein. Villeicht sych Got unser wider erbarmet und ergezt uns wider, nachdem er uns heimgesuget hat. Deucht mich nun, wan du hie, all meins leids desto eh vergesen wolt! Ist mir iezt ein tag so long, als vor 3, wil mich des zu dir versehen, du werst dich vor dem gleidt heraufmachen, wan sein kon. Trag nor zbeifel an dir, wan du aus veter Paulus Scheirels schreiben den leidigen fal vernumen, aug aus disem schreiben, du nimer herauff vor dem gleid werst gedencken. Wil mich aber des besten zu dir versehen. Gott helf uns mit freuden und an mer zuval wider zusamen! Wie den aus deinem schreiben vernumen, das dir Got der herr wol hinabgeholfen hat: der verley eug ein gute mes! Sunst hab in ehrlich zur ertten besteden lasen, als ein amdere leich, an das kein mender leid gewesen ist. Und hat in zu fru nach korleuden hinausgetragen mit dem ganzen cohr und zu fru geleudt." Ibid., p. 169.

102
"recovered from measles [footnote]: May 16, 1594, p. 199.

105
". . . happen now.": "Got ein schmerzlichen ris dorch unser freudt hat thun." Sept. 13, 1592, p. 174.

105
". . . if it were permitted.": "Kind uns wol einen mitdeiln, wens gilte." Ibid.

105
the Jakob Imhoffs.: March 22, 1594, pp. 200–201.

106
". . . a stopped-up liver?": "Am puben seligen wol gesehen, was mit sich pringt, wan die lebern verstofpt ist." Ibid., April 4, 1594, p. 217.

106
". . . helped little Balthasar.": March 22, 1597, p. 280.

106
". . . he is her father.": May 6, 1594, p. 197; June 20, 1594,
pp. 207–8; July 13, 1594, p. 221.

106
buy Madela a dress.: June 26, 1594, p. 213; September 1596,
p. 273.

106
". . . chattering Madela.": "Meiner klein pladereten Madel."
Aug. 1, 1594, pp. 228–29.

106
". . . enjoy her so.": Aug. 29, 1594, p. 242.

107
in his letters.: Apr. 13, 1595, p. 259.

107
". . . letter for her.": April 19, 1596, p. 264.

107
". . . of the staff there.": May 2, 1594, p. 196.

108
his youthful whims.: June 1, 1594, p. 203.

108
secretly laughing.: June 29, 1594, p. 216.

108
". . . satisfied man.": July 13, 1594, p. 222.

108
Balthasar's evaluation.: June 1, 1594, p. 205.

109
also respected.: July 20, 1594, pp. 224–25.

109
wanted to embark.: Sept. 6, 1594, p. 248.

109
". . . than they often get.": "Das sein vatter so hartt gegen
ime, macht vileicht das, das er nit gern wolt, eins umbschlug
under sein kindern. Hets mer manger vater gern, dennoch
offt felt." Aug. 1, 1594, pp. 229–30.


V: Survivors

110
". . . were not so.": July 7, 1584, p. 51.

110
". . . her salvation.": June 24, 1584, p. 210.

110
urinary disease.: Mar. 22, 1591, pp. 110–11.

110
". . . from her mouth.": Oct. 20, 1591, p. 124; Dec. 9, 1591,
p. 142.

110
bottle is opened.: May 15, 1594, p. 199.

110
convulsive death.: September 1596, p. 273.

111
as September 1592.: Sept. 16, 1594, p. 249; Sept. 13, 1592, p. 175.

111
". . . one after the other.": July 18, 1584, p. 54.

111
"greatly depressed.": Nov. 17, 1591, p. 135.

111
Magdalena writes.: Nov. 25, 1591, p. 138.

111
". . . wants something.": Dec. 9, 1591, p. 142.

112
". . . for a long time.": Dec. 23, 1591, p. 144.

112
"took a beautiful end.": Dec. 30, 1591, p. 151.

112
"happy resurrection.": Jan. 1, 1592, p. 153; Jan. 8, 1592, p. 158; Jan. 29, 1592, p. 162.

114
weed out quacks.: *Naturwissenschaft, Medizin und Technik vom 15.–17. Jahrhundert in Nürnberg: Ausstellung der Stadtbibliothek und des Stadtarchivs Nürnberg . . . vom 4. bis 8. Sept. 1967* (Nuremberg, 1967); Egon Philipp, *Das Medizinal- und Apothekenrecht in Nürnberg: Zu seiner Kenntnis von den Anfängen bis zur Gründung des Collegium pharmazeuticum* (1632) (Frankfurt am Main, 1962).

116
". . . our Lord Jesus Christ.": *Ein kurtz Regiment wie man sich in Zeit Regierender Pestilentz halten soll. Durch die Hochgelerten und erfarnen der Ertzney Doctores/Zusammen gefast und gebessert* (Nuremberg, 1562), pp. A 3 b–A 4 a. Reeditions in 1574, 1575, and 1585.

117
". . . the hands of God.": *Anzaig und bericht der Statt Nürnberg verordenten und geschwornen Doctorn der Artzney/die jetzregierende geverliche Haubtkranckheit belangend* (Nürnberg, 1572), pp. B 2 b, D 2 b.

117
charms against disease.: *Ein kurtz Regiment*, p. B 2 b.

118
the physicians warn.: "Ain gar grosser isthumb." *Ibid.*, p. C 2 b.

118
invite illness.: *Ibid.*, p. C 3 b.

118
"anger between us": See above, page 36.

119
". . . as long as I live!": Sept. 2, 9, 1589, pp. 100–101.

119
"something" . . . against "bad air": Sept. 13, 1592, pp. 174–75; September 1596, pp. 168–69.

119
arteries with veins.: Zeeden, *Deutsche Kultur,* p. 300.

119
becomes her plea.: April 19, 1584, p. 42.

120
". . . bad humors there.": Nov. 4, 1591, p. 126. "*Die flis,*" "*Fluess,*" "*fluessig*" are the terms Magdalena and Balthasar use to describe their most persistent and perplexing ailments. The basic term *Fluess* connotes inflammation or a fever that often is accompanied by a "flow" (mucus, phlegm, blood, diarrhea) from one organ (or part of the body) or another. It can describe a runny nose, gout, or rheumatism. See Max Höfler, *Deutsches Krankheitsnamen-Buch* (Munich, 1899), pp. 159–63. Both Magdalena and Balthasar suffer from rheumatism, with Balthasar's chronic intestinal distress their most persistent and baffling ailment. I translate *flis* and related terms, according to context, generally as "bad humors" or "sickly" and more specifically as inflammation, swelling, or rheumatic pain.

120
for good health.: Zeeden, *Deutsche Kultur,* p. 300; *Anzaig und Bericht,* p. B 2 a.

120
never again to procrastinate.: *Briefwechsel,* Nov. 11, 1591, p. 132.

120
in her shoulder.: May 6, 1594, p. 197.

121
wonders of bleeding.: December 1591, p. 149; January 1592, pp. 164–65.

126
". . . against my will.": June 13, 1584, pp. 44–45. On the history of German bath culture in all its ramifications (with pictures), see Alfred Martin, *Deutsches Badewesen in vergangenen Tagen Nebst einem Beitrage zur Geschichte der deutschen Wasserheilkunde* (Jena, 1906).

126
". . . through me.": June 25, 1584, pp. 46–47.

127
". . . his divine will.": July 18, 1584, p. 52.

128
". . . at the mercy of the doctor.": "Des doctors gnaden leben muess." June 5, 1591, p. 113.

128
confined to quarters.: *Ibid.*

128
later than planned.: June 12, 1591, p. 115.

129
hardly detect it.: June 20, 1591, p. 116.

129
"if God is willing.": June 1, 1594, pp. 201–2; June 13, 1594, p. 204.

130
". . . extend his blessing to me.": June 1, 1594, p. 202.

130
". . . a great deal of slime from me.": June 22, 1594, pp. 208, 209.

131
the tedium of his work.: *Ibid.*, p. 209; June 29, 1594, p. 214.

131
". . . to work against me.": June 22, 1594, p. 209.

131
if he so recommends.: June 26, 1594, p. 212; July 10, 1594, p. 219.

131–32
". . . means of preserving you": "Das aber Got dorg dises mitel genetiglich hat verhutten woln, das du hinein bist zogen und so wol gereiniget sunder iezt dorgs waser, wol wir im danken." July 4, 1594, p. 217.

132
". . . until one is well again.": Aug. 1, 1594, p. 226.

132
warmed spring water: Aug. 10, 1594, p. 235–36.

133
whatever he requires.: Aug. 29, 1594, p. 243.

133
". . . in this regard.": Aug. 29, 1594, pp. 245–46.

134
trip to Genoa.: Sept. 6, 1594, pp. 247–48; Sept. 14, 1594, p. 251.

134
bedridden most of the time.: April 23, 1596, pp. 264–65.

VI: BELIEVERS

**136**

from eternity.: Karl Schornbaum, "Nürnberg im Geistesleben des 16. Jahrhunderts. Ein Beitrag zur Geschichte der Konkordienformel," *MVGN* 40 (1949): 40, 50–53; Pfeiffer, ed., *Nürnberg: Geschichte einer europäischen Stadt*, chs. 43, 46; Irmgard Höss, "Das religiös-geistige Leben in Nürnberg am Ende des 15. und am Ausgang des 16. Jahrhunderts," *Miscellanea Historiae Ecclesiasticae*, II, *Congrès de Vienne, Aout-Septembre 1965* (Louvain, 1967), pp. 35–36; Siegfried Scheurl, *Die theologische Fakultät Altdorf im Rahmen der werdenden Universität, 1575–1623* (Nuremberg, 1949).

**137**

covertly and illegally.: Among the laity reported to have joined the services in St. Clara's and St. Katherine's was the great merchant Carl Imhoff. Karl Ulrich, *Die Nürnberger Deutschordens Kommende in ihrer Bedeutung für den Katholizismus seit der Glaubensspaltung* (Kallmünz, 1935), pp. 16–21. Balthasar mentions with alarm Carl Imhoff's bankruptcy in Augsburg in 1594, the only time he appears in the correspondence. *Briefwechsel*, Aug. 3, 1594, p. 232. Magdalena and Balthasar were close to other members of the Imhoff family.

**138**

a breach with the pope.: Lothar Bauer, "Die italienischen Kaufleute und ihre Stellung im protestantischen Nürnberg am Ende des 16. Jahrhunderts (Zu einem Bericht an die Kurie vom Jahre 1593)," *Jahrbuch für fränkische Landesforschung* 22 (1962): 3–7; Ulrich, *Die . . . Deutschordens Kommende*, p. 22.

**142**

repaid in kind.: Bauer, "Die italienischen Kaufleute," 12–13. *Briefwechsel*, March 14, 1589, p. 94; Sept. 12, 1591, p. 122; Aug. 29, 1594, p. 241.

**142**

his business correspondence.: Jan. 1, 1592, pp. 153–54.

**143**

begged him for.: Aug. 1, 1594, p. 230.

**143**

". . . danced before.": "Bin gester erigtag auf des Schmitmers hondschlag gewesen, von herzen langweilig, das mon so lang gedichst und so ser gedruncken die mender, das mich teucht, nit so sund wer, mon davir gedanzt hete." July 10, 1594, p. 220.

**143**

". . . pay the church for it.": September 1596, p. 273.

144
in both lands.: Nov. 9, 1591, p. 131.

144
". . . abuse wine so outrageously.": Sept. 1, 1596, p. 269.

144
". . . for her untrue heart": Sept. 8, 1590, p. 106; March
1591, p. 110–11; March 22, 1591, p. 111.

144
dies in Lyon.: Dec. 15, 1582, p. 9.

145
Frau Georg Volckamer.: Aug. 8, 1584, p. 61.

145
". . . resurrection in Christ.": Jan. 29, 1592, p. 162 (third
time).

145
seems to deserve.: July 1, 1584, p. 48.

145
". . . have ended.": "Also inn summa inn dieser weltt eben
nichtts bestendigs, darumb wir ia billig viel mehr auf das
ewige weder zeittliche bauen sollenn." July 18, 1594, p. 54.

145
". . . on human help.": "Auf menschhilff bauen." Aug. 8,
1594, p. 61.

146
". . . do so still again.": Jan. 1, 1583, p. 18.

146
". . . back to me in joy . . .": July 7, 1584, p. 50.

146
". . . knowing such pain.": March 22, 1591, p. 111.

146
dying from gangrene.: May 16, 1594, p. 199.

146
"end it soon": Dec. 9, 1591, p. 142.

147
". . . such a calamity.": Jan. 6, 1592, p. 155.

147
". . . his divine will.": Aug. 8, 1584, p. 59; Aug. 14, 1584,
p. 62.

147
God gets the credit.: Sept. 17, 1588, p. 92.

147
". . . that much longer.": June 1, 1594, p. 203.

148
". . . surrender ourselves.": March 15, 1592, p. 170.

148
parts of Franconia.: Hartmut H. Kunstmann, *Zauberwahn
und Hexenprozess in der Reichsstadt Nürnberg* (Nuremberg,
1970), pp. 182–84.

149
". . . much less in theirs.": *Grundtlicher Berich/Was von der Zauberei und Hexenwerck zu halten sei: Ein hellige Antwort der hochgelehrten Theologen und Predicanten zu Nuremberg* (1613), appended to Antonius Praetorius, *Von Zauberei und Zauberern* (1613), pp. 325–26. Copy in The British Library.

149
". . . and for the best.": *Ibid.*, pp. 333–34.

150
weekday prayer vigils.: *Briefwechsel*, Sept. 17, 1592, p. 177.

150
migrating geese.: May 16, 1594, p. 199; June 20, 1594, p. 207; June 26, 1594, p. 213; July 4, 1594, p. 217; Sept. 12, 1594, p. 250; Sept. 8, 1594, p. 253; Sept. 28, 1594, p. 256.

150
"better a plague . . .": "Got behut vir sterbsleift! Doch was Got wil: wer noch beser ein sterb, dan der turck." Sept. 17, 1592, p. 177.

150
". . . often need it.": March 23, 1588, p. 86.

150
a German Bible.: April 12, 1596, p. 261.

151
". . . cries of war.": Sept. 18, 1594, p. 253.

151
". . . the small children.": Sept. 12, 1594, p. 250.

151
". . . with the guilty.": Aug. 8, 1594, p. 233.

154
". . . provide also for yourself.": "Der allmechttig ewige Gott wölle zu allem gnade, glück, segen unnd gedeyen geben unnd mitthailn, du aber wöllest inndessen deiner auch schonen unnd zu widerwerttigkeitt selber nitt ursach gebenn, alls ich mich dann zu dir versehen will, du von selber thon werdest." July 18, 1584, p. 53.

155
an ailing horse.: "Es mus doch umer etwas uberzberg goh." Oct. 20, 1591, p. 124. Theodor Hampe includes a short letter of Magdalena's to her brother Paul among his survey of "Sprichwörter, Redensarten, Witz und Schilderung in altnürnberger Briefen," *MVGN* 31 (1933): 165–205.

156
". . . the same for a long time.": Oct. 20, 1591, p. 124.

156
". . . which is true.": Dec. 1, 1591, p. 140.

157
on the bed.: Jan. 6, 1592, p. 155; Jan. 13, 1592, p. 164.

157
Jakob Imhoff's family.: Dec. 25, 1582, p. 15; Sept. 18, 1594, p. 255.

157
". . . every way one can.": Dec. 25, 1591, p. 145.

158
famine, plague, or war.: Endres, "Einwohnerzahl," 264, 266–68.

159
while singing psalms.: Smith, "Description," 230.

159
". . . reward he deserves.": "Er wiert einmal sein lon empfangen, wiers verdindt." March 22, 1597, p. 280.

159
". . . it still has its promise.": "Es sei halt etwas so klein es wel, iezt so hat es das gereis." April 1595, p. 260.

160
". . . the money I have lost.": Sept. 6, 1594, p. 249.


VII: FAMILIES PAST AND PRESENT

162
"from patriarchy to partnership.": Michael Mitterauer and Reinhard Sieder, *Vom Patriarchat zur Partnerschaft: Zum Strukturwandel der Familie* (Munich, 1977); English edition: *The European Family: Patriarchy to Partnership, from the Middle Ages to the Present* (Chicago, 1983).


EPILOGUE

165
"together in Holenstein.": March 22, 1597, p. 281.

166
". . . in the kitchen.": Dec. 11, 1598, p. 284.

# ⧨ABOUT
# THE AUTHOR

Steven Ozment, professor of history at Harvard University and associate dean for undergraduate education there, is a widely respected leading cultural historian of the Reformation. He is the author of *The Age of Reform*—nominated in 1981 for the American Book Award and winner of the Philip Schaff History Prize of the American Society of Church History—has written six scholarly books, and is coauthor of two best-selling history texts. His most recent book is *When Fathers Ruled: Family Life in Reformation Europe*. Professor Ozment lives with his family in Newbury, Mass.